Philosophy, Science and the

Sociology of Knowledge

PHILOSOPHY, SCIENCE AND THE SOCIOLOGY OF KNOWLEDGE

By
IRVING LOUIS HOROWITZ
Professor of Sociology and Political Science
Rutgers University

With a Foreword by
Robert S. Cohen
Chairman, Department of Physics
Boston University

GREENWOOD PRESS, PUBLISHERS
WESTPORT CONNECTICUT

301.21
H81p

Library of Congress Cataloging in Publication Data

Horowitz, Irving Louis.
Philosophy, science, and the sociology of knowledge.

Reprint of the 1961 ed. published by Thomas, Springfield, Ill., which was issued as publication no. 442 of American lecture series.
Includes bibliographical references and indexes.
1. Knowledge, Sociology of. I. Title.
[BD175.H65 1976]   301.2'1   76-27756
ISBN 0-8371-9051-7

© *1961, by* CHARLES C THOMAS ● PUBLISHER

m.R.

Originally published in 1961 by Charles C Thomas, Publisher, Springfield, Illinois

Reprinted with the permission of Charles C Thomas, Publisher

Reprinted in 1976 by Greenwood Press, a division of Congressional Information Service, 88 Post Road West, Westport, Connecticut 06881

Library of Congress catalog card number 76-27756.

ISBN 0-8371-9051-7

Printed in the United States of America

10 9 8 7 6 5 4 3 2

Preface

When we pause to consider the long haul involved in getting from raw experience to knowledge—the gathering, recording, sorting, analysis, ordering, diffusion, and correlation of data; and then at another stage, the formation of hypotheses, concepts and laws—it becomes perfectly clear that knowledge is not so much wished for as worked for. Because knowledge is so precious an item, it should be jealously prized and no less carefully appraised. For with so much sifting of primary information, one must wonder why, once knowledge is attained, so many conflicting claims are made on its behalf. And yet the history of scientific discovery offers abundant evidence that its claims are repeatedly challenged; challenges which increase in ferocity and intensity the nearer science comes to the study of men and societies. It is not my purpose to cast doubt on any branch of science or knowledge in general. What I am interested in showing are the conditions under which, and the social positions through which, knowledge is bent to serve human interests first and truth second; and parallel to this, the social forces and factors which enable these same human interests to be able to pursue the search for truth without bias.

In order to satisfactorily treat one segment of the problem of knowledge, I will examine the present status of the relationship of modern philosophy to the sociology of knowledge. It has long been apparent that a close historical tie exists. Every pioneer in the sociology of knowledge had clear philosophic antecedents. Weber and Scheler, despite different religious backgrounds, were neo-Kantians. Mannheim's link to a naturalistic Hegelianism served as his constant point of departure. Nor is this a strictly European phenomenon. Veblen cut his first intellectual teeth on the works of Kant, while more recently the pragmatism of Dewey helped shape the structural-functional school of Merton and Parsons. And Adler (1957) has recently shown the degree to which

v

problems in and attitudes toward the sociology of knowledge have been shaped by appraisals of the work of Marx.

For their part, such major figures in the history of philosophy as Plato, Bacon, Hume, and Helvetius anticipated the independent study of the social conditioning of ideas through such studies as the role of myths, idols and interests in shaping the human view of reality. However, although historical examinations of the pre-history of the sociology of knowledge have been made by Grün-wald (1934), Dahlke (1940), Barth (1945), Maquet (1949), and Stark (1958), little has been done on the relation of the two fields from an analytic perspective.

I propose therefore to emphasize the analytical issues: the relation of the sociology of knowledge to established philosophic schools; the connection between epistemology and the social sources of human consciousness; the link between general ideas and particular ideologies; the sociology of knowledge treated as a behavioral science; and the philosophical implications of conflicting tendencies in the sociology of knowledge.

The major task I have set for myself is to distinguish the sociology of knowledge from both its philosophic ancestry and from behavioral psychology, the two fields which are closest in concern to the sociology of knowledge. My contention is that such distinctions can be fruitfully made, and must be made, if the social dimension of ideas is to be pursued as an independent discipline. (Cf. Znaniecki, 1951). In sharpening the contents and limits of this recent addition to the empirical sciences, philosophy and logic perform a crucial function of providing meaning and significance to an area which thus far has been hindered in its evolution by linguistic snags, national idosyncrasies, and ambiguous and sometimes treacherous political rivalries.

Clearly, so brief a study can but introduce the main themes and offer only tentative conclusions. For those who would admonish me for not offering an exhaustive account of one problem instead of a broad account of several problems, I can only repeat the words of Marianne Weber (1921) concerning her husband's efforts: "Was ich nicht mache, machen andere."

This monograph grew out of lectures and courses on the sociology of knowledge first delivered at the University of Buenos

Aires, and later at Bard College. To the students and other participants in these lectures goes my first and deepest thanks. A special note of appreciation is due to Professor Gino Germani, director of the Institute of Sociology in the University of Buenos Aires, who first perceived the value of an enterprise attempting to bridge the gap between the sociology of knowledge and social philosophy. The monograph itself was considerably enhanced by Professor Marvin Farber's suggestion that there be a section on the pre-history of the sociology of knowledge, and also a glossary of some of the more obscure terms used. Professor Robert S. Cohen of Boston University read the manuscript with his customary critical discernment. Because of him, the manuscript undoubtedly contains far fewer errors of omission and commission than would otherwise have been the case. Professor Franz Adler of Los Angeles State College, Professor Paul Honigsheim of Michigan State University, and Professor Daniel J. Levinson of Harvard University, each placed valuable unpublished materials at my disposal which considerably eased my tasks.

I. L. H.

Foreword

Irving Louis Horowitz has written, in *Philosophy, Science and the Sociology of Knowledge,* of the interesting but puzzling relation between the sociology of thought and philosophical analysis of thought. Thought is cognitive; it can be true, but is more often false. Thought is also social; in origin, development, function, and pre-suppositions, it reveals the thinker and his situation. Finally, thoughts have their meaning both because of experience of the world and because of patterns of interpretation, which in turn can be investigated analytically or culturally. From sociology may come knowledge of what in society determines what in thought. From philosophical analysis may come critical understanding of the tests of validity. And one may expect that a sociological theory of knowledge will explain how it is that an individual thinker, in his time, place, and person, is enabled to think with ascertainable degrees of validity and within an epistemological framework of concepts and categories. Why do men project and believe illusions? How do they reach truth?

In the account which is offered in *Philosophy, Science and the Sociology of Knowledge,* we have the clearest brief exposition of the connection between sociology of knowledge and general sociology, between sociology of knowledge and general epistemological theories, between sociology of knowledge as European and as American. The range is vast for it must be a historical account of the awareness of the limitations upon thought and yet it must be a contemporary critical analysis of the empirical theories of knowledge. Professor Horowitz explores both directions of this range, and he goes further in decisively setting forth certain central open questions. Thus, we have no longer the task of defining terms but rather of evolving a working, a scientific, methodology of investigation. Furthermore, we recognize that there are sociologies of knowledge, not in the sense of alternative conceptual schemes but rather in the sense of apparently distinct realms of knowledge; for there are cognitive claims to be made for religion, music, art, literature, law, philosophy itself, as well as for science, and hence the sociology of each much separately pose the question of relating the sociology of knowledge to the sociological analysis of culture. Finally, we confront a critical test of this new science of knowledge: can we learn to predict the assertive statements and ideological claims of representative members of human social groups? Can we recommend which policies will bring about the flourishing of valid knowledge, in the diverse social and economic realities of the present world? Can we account, with plausible argument and evidence, for the cognitive systems of other times than our own?

A theory which can be used to formulate confirmable predictions must itself be scientific, and in Horowitz's view, it cannot, therefore, be ideological. Science and ideology, however much they mix as components of thought, are antithetical. Science, in this view, is objective, the same for each observer, whatever his political or economic position. Ideology is subjective, bound to and distorted by the personal, social, economic and historical situation of the thinker, and hence it is a prejudiced and self-serving enterprise of thought, which is always connected with the advancement of particular interests. Thus, theology, a system of thought, may be seen as the ideology of religion, a social institution.

This distinction is clear enough in statement but not obvious in application. What is science to one group turns out to be ideology to another. Disentangling the ideological elements in thoughts from the scientific, the *seinsgebunden* from the *wertfrei*, is as difficult as distinguishing conventional elements from empirical. Moreover, it is natural to recognize that truth, objective truth, serves some interests at some times. Then it is liberating. At other times, it may be corrosive to the same particular interests. If we consider that truth, half-truth, error, and illusion, each have their social function and their cognitive claim, we can offer an alternative to Professor Horowitz's usage: all thought is ideological for all thought is functional in a social sense. When the situation of a thinker promotes objective and confirmable thinking, to that extent do man's thoughts become scientific, and to that extent his is a scientific ideology. Ideology will be transcended only when all our interests are served solely by objective investigation, when human prejudice causes a universal abandonment of partisan prejudice. Until then, it is quite the same type of question, to ask, under what conditions, truth is attainable, as to ask, under what conditions, illusion is attainable. Only the answers may differ; and we must be both modest and cautious in judging truth-discovering, truth-creating, truth-recognizing properties of advanced society, the society which has nourished science.

The sociological and comparative study of knowledge in all its forms joins with one traditional motivation of religious prophecy and classical philosophy, the critical attempt to bring thinking out of sectarian pride, to transcend each socio-centric predicament, especially our own. In this sense, Professor Horowitz has thought through a sharply discerning argument which deserves appreciative scrutiny and invites discussion. I hope that scientists of all disciplines as well as philosophers will recognize the importance of his work.

PROFESSOR ROBERT S. COHEN
Chairman, Department of Physics
Boston University

Contents

*Philosophy, Science and the
Sociology of Knowledge*

Chapter I

The Scientific Study of Knowledge: Challenge and Response

Тне efforts to realize a general theory of knowledge that can direct us when we have genuine information about external reality, an undertaking begun in ancient China and Greece, remains a goal sought rather than an achievement registered. Just when men become certain they have distinguished the true path from the false, as in enlightenment theories of the progress of mind and society, a doubt begins to engulf them. The rationalist vision of a Condorcet becomes an intellectual embarrassment rather than a contribution of the philosopher to social progress; a babbling agglomeration of philosophers rather than a liberating community of men. Not only are scientific explanations of human events held up to ridicule, but more important, the intrinsic value of such an enterprise is itself considered futile.

The scientific mind is confronted with Dostoevsky's (1864) sick, spiteful and unattractive "underground man." At that very moment in the nineteenth century when Comte, Huxley, Marx and Mill were predicting the widest possibilities of the human control of society, the literary existentialists reminded man of his irrational core. Dostoevsky shook his finger at science which pretends to pure rational necessities. 'It is just a man's fantastic dreams, his vulgar folly that he will desire to retain, simply in order to prove himself—as though that were necessary—that men still are men and not the keys of a piano, which the laws of nature threaten to control so completely that soon one will be able to desire nothing but by the calendar."

The nineteenth century man of science, haunted by the romantic literati, responded to the challenge long enough to note that

3

human beings need not be treated as automata in the search to explain social change. What they could not do is provide a rational explanation of irrationality. This achievement belongs to the *fin de siècle* and the work of Poincaré in mathematics, Durkheim in sociology and Freud in psychology. It was from then on that scientists have been able to point out to irrationalist critics that a universe of caprice and free-will creates a world no less unbearable than Huxley's mechanically perfect *Brave New World* and rationally less plausible. The fears of scientism had to be put aside in order to create a branch of sociology which would explain the social conditions in which knowledge is attainable, and no less important, the phenomena which lead to the distortion of knowledge.

The sociology of knowledge acquired status as an independent discipline by examining the social channels through which knowledge, whether it be termed propagandistic or scientific, is filtered. As Adler (1957), Kaufman (1944), and Merton (1957) have noted, despite certain national differences, the sociology of knowledge operated within the generally established rules used by the other behavioural sciences. This is not to discount differences between intuitive-individualist approaches prominent in Central Europe, and empirical-cooperative attitudes evolved in the United States. But new possibilities of translating the work of one into the other, has overcome much of the earlier difficulties scholars had in working with the sociology of knowledge (Wolff, 1959).

But at this juncture, the sociologist exploring knowledge is again confronted by critics who doubt the ultimate efficacy of the enterprise. After all, who can really say that science is itself an inviolable method for testing everything except the axiological system upon which its supremacy is established? Critics like Jaspers (1955) come to the foreground and formalize the fragments of the metaphysics Dostoevsky left behind. "The cogent correctness of the sciences is but a small part of truth. This correctness, in its universal validity, does not unite us completely as real human beings, but only as intellectual beings. It unites us in the object that is understood in the particular, but not in the totality."

This type of charge must be faced directly by the sociology of knowledge, since it is that discipline which attempts to show men in their mental relation to social history and to their immediate circumstances. Is science but a small and perishable part of the truth as Jaspers says? What are the means for verifying these larger truths? If science is a total approach to truth, what accounts for the growth of transcendental theories of truth? What are the social sources of the division of man into intellectuals and practitioners? Does a division of the world into inanimate objects and feeling subjects foster artificial interest roles in society? Do dualisms of head and hand, mind and body, spirit and matter, perpetuate social myths, or do they perform antiseptic roles in preventing science from becoming dizzy with success? The very ability to ask such questions and to ascertain the contradictory social goals towards which doctrines tend, indicates that the sociology of knowledge is a scientific tool and not a speculative conquest.

If we wish to think as social scientists, we are no longer confronted with systematic philosophies vying with each other, but rather with the analysis of the social import and impact of all forms of knowledge (including systems and anti-systems in philosophy). The consequence of viewing knowledge as a problem rather than as heuristically given, is a distinctive dimension of the social sciences. Through this dimension, a sound reply to the adversaries of contemporary science can be framed, based upon factual observation and causal explanation.

The transformation of knowledge from a fact of reflection into a problem for self-reflection has rich historical antecedents. This change coincides with the recognition that the social conditioning of human mental processes constitutes a unique area of cognitive inquiry, quite apart from the study of action situations. Earlier philosophic contributions to this area, while clearing a path for putting the problem of knowledge on a social footing, lacked a scientific method for converting their criticisms of metaphysical formulas into an examination of the laws governing the relations of human thought to social action. The sociology of knowledge defined for the first time the initial and limiting conditions of the social components of thought.

The view that metaphysical formulas cannot rise above broad

moral imperatives (cf. Ayer, 1936; and Hare, 1952), into the actual functioning of knowledge in a social context, has produced a veritable revolution in philosophy. The charge that science, in examining details, offers little prospect for an overall human frame of reference, simply ignores the facts. The recent cooperative efforts edited by Grinker (1956), Adorno (1950), and Christie and Jahoda (1954) indicate a clear awareness of the need for science to provide more substance in the way of a general theory of human behavior. Simply because these new efforts at a scientific synthesis have not been unanimously accepted, even by the participants in these colloquia, is no reason to disparage the capacity of science to frame general laws about man. The intuitionist urge to break rules and avoid methodological scrutiny is not a faster way to truth, but only illustrates the metaphysical propensity to transcend all rules. It is what Dewey (1929) described as the substitution of the search for meaning, a false quest for certainty. The intensive efforts to work out a general theory of human behavior, social theories of why men act, interdisciplinary activities to account for situations at the borderland of older sciences, the clarification of the language of science, indicate that synthesis can no longer be conceived as the private property of gifted metaphysicians.

The special dimension of metaphysical doctrines has always rested upon the inviolability and mystery of the human mind— its uniqueness among all things in the cosmos, its ability to comprehend uncomprehending things. Jaspers (1955) notes that Kierkegaard was astonished at the optimism pervading the man of science. "They do not experience the maturity of that critical point where everything turns upside down." Surely, Jaspers well knows that scientific statements have been upset many times, as the history of physics from Copernicus to Einstein illustrates. What seems really at stake is the persistent idea that progress in the sciences is nonetheless possible. What separates the scientific view from other positions is Jaspers' further claim that "one understands more and more that there is something which one cannot understand." Science is indeed limited. But it does not convert its limits into fetishes. The unknown exists as the yet to be known, not as in the case of *Existenzphilosophie,* something never to be known.

In the *fin de siècle* realization that mind (even irrational mind) is itself an object for social study and not merely an agency for describing objects, can be located the genesis of both psycho-analysis and the sociology of knowledge. The former defines the limits of normality in terms of how accurately individuals are capable of representing and resolving the problems of the external world. The latter is concerned with knowledge from a social vantage point, that is, the accuracy with which social strata and economic classes represent the world. In the transformation of thinking process from a constant into a variable, from a static factor in the biological hierarchy into an analysable element in the social structure, we are able to trace the foundations and limits of *Wissenssoziologie.*

The sociology of knowledge has as a minimum base the attempt to eliminate indeterminism from the social context of idea forma-tion. It is unwarranted to assume that the existence of irrational behavior is proof of indeterminism. Quite the contrary, the classi-fication of types of irrational behavior by psychiatry, sociology and political science, is evidence that scientific determinations can be established. Of course, the social study of knowledge is com-plicated. The investigator must be aware, among other things, of the fact that any social event can have non-repeating character-istics; that the distinction between facts, norms and values is ex-tremely difficult to segregate; that for the most part the sociology of knowledge is itself bound to the vagaries of ordinary language systems; and that the investigator must account for socially bound distortions in his own thinking, and adjust for them in a rather makeshift fashion. Add to these the historical problems inherited from metaphysical systems, and one can readily see just how de-manding the area is upon the serious investigator.

The first step in defining the content of the sociology of knowl-edge is to make clear what it is not. In the first place, it is not epistemology; for it is not so much concerned with the accuracy with which men represent reality, but the social categories which make questions of matter and mind political questions.

Discussions concerning the superiority of the correspondence or coherence theories of truth are limited to the forms in which knowledge arises. They tell us little of the content, and nothing of the context, of knowledge. It is when the need to satisfy contextual problems becomes pressing that the sociology of knowledge arises. It probes the content of ideas by revealing the social matrix of truth and error, validation and speculation. It may show, as Merton (1957) in his paradigms for functionalism and the sociology of knowledge, how a given social group comes to accept or reject epistemological criteria. It may further reveal the types of epistemologies preferred by different professional groups. (Cf. Adler, 1954; Pribram, 1949.) The sociology of knowledge benefits from epistemology in being clear as to its hypothetical and axiological dealings, and in stating its operative base in terms of philosophic criteria of significance and meaning. The more explicit the reciprocity of sociology and philosophy at this level the wider the possibilities of linking facts and their meanings.

The advantage of the sociology of knowledge for the behavioural sciences stems from its unique task of separating truth functions from ideological functions—not that *historically* speaking they can be isolated. However, social science is faced with a serious problem of choice. We need only consider the alternative approaches taken to the legacy left by Plato, Aristotle or Spinoza, or the contradictory conclusions reached in the study of such historic events as the Protestant Reformation or the French Revolution, to see how profound a factor ideological commitments have been in the study of both social and intellectual history. The social sciences, however institutionally supported, would be incomplete without accounting for or adjusting the bias of the man of learning. This does not convert the sociology of knowledge into a "thorough-going historical relativism" as Aron (1935) claims. It simply means that truth does not spring up from the brain of its discoverer pure and pristine, free of distortion. In short, the process of science is itself sociological in character. And the work of such historians of science as Bachelard (1957), Butterfield (1949), Needham (1956), and Bernal (1954) takes this conclusion out of a speculative realm.

Conversely, institutional elements are the material preconditions of knowledge. The sociologist can no more estimate distortions in the knowing process without a working conception of economics, psychology and political science, than the man of medicine can study disturbances in the central nervous system without a knowledge of at least physiology and organic chemistry. The study of how men receive and employ knowledge involves a perspective as to the worth of given bodies of information. Even in defining the initial and limiting conditions of the sociology of knowledge, it already points beyond itself towards the interrelation of the social sciences.

In sum, the most widely repeated arguments against the social determination of ideas is: first, no scientific index includes all the factors that affect thought; and second, there are individual differences in personal reaction to systems of knowledge. But granting these points, one cannot declare a social explanation of ideas useless merely by stating the existence of these problems. The usefulness of an index, whether statistical, historical or functional, is determined by how much information it yields in spite of the "human factors," and the convenience of computation. The spoken word is a useful index to our thoughts and emotions despite the obvious imperfection of ordinary language and the variability in meaning from person to person. What language does, and what symbolic languages try to do better, is reduce the number of factors in representing a complex process such as the interaction of science and social forces. Language further expresses information about interaction, about processes of growth and transformation, even about those processes of thought that are so complex as to appear to be random and capricious. The sociology of knowledge should thus be measured by its successes in reducing caprice, not by the fuel it has supplied to metaphysical critics.

Chapter II

The Pre-History of the Sociology
of Knowledge

The establishment of a new discipline always introduces as an afterthought the search for the historical antecedents.
The sociology of knowledge is no exception to this rule, as the
work of its pioneers show. In this brief discussion, I will not so
much concentrate on personal influences, as on the influence of
certain schools of philosophy. It is, for our purposes, not so important to note when a word was coined, or by whom on what date,
as it is to gain a perspective on the philosophical cross-currents
that pushed social thought from a rationalist to a critical and
scientific orientation. It will become manifestly clear that this
examination of philosophic antecedents is not simply informative,
but more significantly, to show that past philosophical differences
and disputes (in style as well as content) still plague sociologists
of knowledge.

This pre-history does not include later nineteenth century figures like Marx, Dilthey and Nietzsche. Several reasons, other than
the obvious one of space limitations, suggest themselves. First,
Marx's separation of the ideological conscience from conscious deception marks the decisive break with the pre-historic stage of the
sociology of knowledge. However one feels about Mannheim's
contributions to the field, his comment that "the sociology of
knowledge actually emerged with Marx" cannot seriously be disputed. (Cf. Mannheim, 1929; ch. V.) As for Dilthey, it has clearly
been shown by Mandelbaum (1938), Hodges (1944, 1952),
Groethuysen (1913, 1927), Misch (1925), and Horkheimer
(1939), that his roots are embedded in problems raised by the
rationalist methodology of Kant and Hegel, and that even his dis-

tinction between *Geisteswissenschaften* and *Naturwissenschaften* is clearly implied in Hegel's distinction between Mind and Nature. As for Nietzsche, it is certain that he is the great fountainhead of the study of the irrational impulses (crystallized into ideologies) which generate action. In Sorel, Mosca and Pareto a great deal of Nietzsche's work is refracted into the study of mass motivation and social neurosis. The main reason, therefore, that makes a separate examination of the history of the sociology of knowledge unnecessary, is that much of our analysis will concern ideas forged by Marx, Dilthey and Nietzsche—and their successors, Mannheim, Weber and Scheler.

TAOISM AND CONFUCIANISM

Hegel (1833) was never more wrong than when he wrote that our appreciation of Chinese thought "has largely diminished through a further knowledge of it." While any beginning ascribed to the sociological study of ideas has an arbitrary element, there are at least three sound reasons for beginning with ancient Chinese thought. It introduces the notion that knowledge is relative and human understanding finite; it is the first civilization to announce the duality of society and nature; its various branches all agree that the moral is not what men strive for, but rather that what men strive for is termed the moral. The *Jen Wu Chih* of Liu Shao (1937) illustrates these three themes so well, it is worth quoting the original at some length.

"At first, men are hard to know. But everyone thinks that he is able to know men. Therefore when one looks at men by comparison with oneself, they may be considered knowable. But when we see men examining other men, we may conclude that knowledge is not obtained. Why? Because a man can know the goodness that is like his own, but he may lose beauty which is of a different kind." After contrasting the legalist and the strategist, the instrumentalist and the intuitionist, the analyst and the rhetorician, Liu Shao concludes that "all these men contradict one another, and no one is willing to admit that the others are right. When they are dealing with their own kind, they will understand one another at the first meeting. When they are dealing with a different kind of man from themselves they cannot comprehend one another, although they may be together for a long time."

As Needham has indicated (1956), Taoism in particular made a substantial contribution to the relation of knowledge and social institutions. This is because the observation and learning from nature is a precondition to scientific effort. It represents what Needham calls the "thread of empiricism which was of capital importance for the whole development of science and technology in China."

Chuang-Tzu took a position of extreme relativism which nonetheless illustrates Needham's point. He insisted that knowledge of society is akin to dreams; in neither case is the knowledge gleaned a precise representation of reality. "When people dream they do not know that they are dreaming. In their dreams they may even interpret dreams. Only when they wake they begin to know that they dreamed. By and by comes the great awakening, and then we shall find out that life itself is a great dream. All the while the fools think that they are awake, and that they have knowledge." (Cf. Needham, 1956: II:10:f.) Lin Ching-Hsi offered one of the first formulations of the doctrine of *tabula rasa* made famous in the eighteenth century by John Locke. But beyond his contributions to epistemology, Ching-Hsi noted that "once the mind has received impressions of natural things, they tend to remain and not to disappear, thus leaving traces in the mind. These affect later seeing and thinking, so that the mind is not truly 'empty' and unbiased." (Cf. Needham, *ibid.*) Taoism then, was profoundly committed to the view that all knowledge, speculative and empirical, is externally framed if not limited.

Derk Bodde (1957) has noted that the skeptical humanist branch of Confucianism was no less emphatic than Taoism in distinguishing between the operations of nature and those of society on the minds of men (with differing moral stress on the relative virtues of nature and society). Perhaps the earliest formulation of a sociology of religion was made by Hsun-Tzu. He distinguished between prayer and phenomenon. Since no necessary conection between the two can be established, Hsun-Tzu concluded that prayer is "only to make a fine appearance"; a point Hume reiterated in eighteenth century England. The knowing individual will thus view rituals as a gloss over things, while the ignorant man will consider accidental results of praying a supernatural intervention. (Cf. Bodde, 1957:26.) It is important to note that neither Taoism nor Confucianism expressed doubt as to the existence of an external reality, or the cumulative nature of observing and thinking. What was expressed was doubt that men having inherited religious bias, can represent reality with fidelity.

To give some idea of the scope of the Chinese contribution to a social theory of ideas, we might mention the work of such diverse figures as Motse and Han Fei Tzu. The former, a contemporary of Confucius, offered the first calculus for testing social propositions. It was based on the Idea of Universal Good. The moral measuring device was, however, quite utilitarian. Good is based on what is useful; and utility is in turn tested by past experience, present experience, and the effects of ideas on people. To this Motse joined the principle of economy. Things were to be tested by their contribution to the social order, social justice, and the social economy. In this way, War would be ruled evil since it fails to meet the test of utility and the principle of economy (or better, conservation). (Cf. Bogardus, 1940.)

Han Fei Tzu, whom Waley (1939) calls a "realist," is indeed an unusual figure. Unlike any of the other schools of thought, realism sharply separated an understanding of mind from the moral purposes it sets for itself. Concerned as it was with the arts of ruling, realism anticipated the Machiavellian analysis of the effects power has over the minds of both ruler and ruled. And in his work, Han Fei Tzu provides a set of non-moral lessons for the understanding of the mind of the ruler, among which are knowing how to adopt one's arguments to the ruler's state of mind, how to flatter without becoming obvious, and conversely, how to criticize without getting into danger. Also examined is the role of secrecy in the art of political rule, the role of deceit in gaining alliances, and the function of the political elite in forming the mental climate of society as a whole. The historic controversy between social order and individual rights firmly divided believers in feudalism, bureaucracy and authoritarianism (Confucians and Legalists), from their chief ideological opponents who believed in pacifism, individualism and the scientific way (Taoists, Mohists and Logicians). But in terms of the evolution of sociological theory, Chinese thought as a whole made a profound contribution to the study of the social, religious and psychological reasons for distortion of ideas.

Although Chinese philosophy reached a high degree of sophistication in distinguishing society from nature, its contribution was circumscribed by being unable to conceive of society as anything more than an enlarged family unit. (Cf. Bodde, 1957:49.) It was left to classical Greek thought to distinguish types of social organization apart from the nuclear family.

PLATO AND LUCRETIUS

Much of the impact of Plato's dialogues on our contemporaries is derived from the thoroughly human terms in which epistemology is examined. The role of knowledge in the formation of theories of justice, principles of government, moral rules, psychological needs and wants, help account for the continuing technical as well as popular interest in his work. Plato's social theories have been examined too often and too well to need summarizing. I shall thus confine myself to seeing how Plato's distinction between image and reality, and the correlate political doctrine of mass and elite, helped to shape modern sociological interpretations of the problem of knowledge.

In the Seventh Book of the *Republic,* Plato (1892a) introduces the problem of moving from the darkness of ignorance to the light of truth. This process is not simply one of education or of instruction, but more profoundly, a matter of psychology. For once the shadow men inhabiting the caves of ignorance are released from the bondage of false images, they do not respond positively and automatically to true knowledge. Quite the opposite occurs. As a result of his socially conditioned state of ignorance, ordinary man rejects the bright light of truth. "At first, when any of them is liberated and compelled suddenly to stand up and turn his neck round and walk and look towards the light, he will suffer sharp pains; the glare will distress him, and he will be unable to see the realities of which in his former state he had seen the shadows; and then conceive someone saying to him, that what he saw before was an illusion, but that now, when he is approaching nearer to being and his eye is turned towards more real existence, he has a clearer vision—what will be his reply?" Plato answers with a question. "Will he not fancy that the shadows which he formerly saw are truer than the objects which are now shown to him?" Thus Plato envisions a "rugged ascent" to truth, an ascent complicated by the difficulties imposed by distinctions of social class.

Knowledge, for Plato, while eternally and absolutely fixed in the firmaments, is not open to all in an equal way. Those who are finally able "to see the sun" rather than mere reflections, are few. Among the reasons given for this are that the mass of men inhabit a sensory world solely; only the few possess the capacity of rational understanding. Lower class strivings are limited to transient passions and material desires. Only the liquidation of these lower strivings, and their replacement with rational wants, can open to man a knowledge of truth and its moral properties. "The prison-house is the world of sight, the light of the fire is the sun, and you will not misapprehend me if you interpret the journey upwards to be the ascent of the soul into the intellectual world according to my poor belief. . . . In the world of knowledge the idea of good appears last of all, and is seen only with an effort." (*Ibid.*, p. 776.) Morals are therefore not something framed in experience, as they are for Chinese philosophy, but a fixed property of truth which an intellectual elite strives to know and interpret.

Exactly how Plato correlates social class and level of attainable knowledge is still a hotly contested question among interpreters like Popper (1952), Wild (1953), Winspear (1940), and Levinson (1953). The degree of interpretive variance suggests that modern disputants are themselves suffering from severe cases of ideological distortion. What is not open to dispute is that Plato establishes a criterion of knowledge that is not equally open to all. Knowledge presupposes a level of intellectual attainment *and* social positioning without which, in Plato's thought, no distinction between illusion and reality would be possible.

The rough correlation between an economic aristocracy and knowledge of truth is, *from a functional viewpoint,* not radically different from the Marxian attempt to frame an inverse correlation of a science of society with the special insights of the leadership of an industrial proletariat. Similarly, Plato, in the *Phaedrus* (1892b) formulated a theory of myths, that is, "the comprehension of scattered particulars in one idea," as a means of insuring control of power by an aristocratic elite; and this in the hands of Sorel (1907, 1908) became a means of galvanizing the masses into revolutionary action. The important point is that, however we view the moral worth of the masses, the role of an elite in manipulating their behaviour has been recognized as indispensable to the social study of ideas. In thus formulating a theory of knowledge in terms of social divisions, and not only as a problem in perception, Plato placed all subsequent social philosophy in his debt.

This granted, it does not exclude the fact that Plato spoke as an ideological representative of his class; with definite interests in maintaining the noble lie as mental nourishment for the masses. It was at this sensitive point that Epicurus and his great Roman follower, Lucretius, made a serious incursion into elitist premises. Taking Lucretius' *De Rerum Natura* (1951) as a faithful representation of the Epicurean philosophy, and it is difficult to draw any other conclusions from the fragments of Epicurus we have, then there is no question that Lucretius directs his social theories against Platonism. As Farrington has observed (1939), "Lucretius did not merely make his position clear as against contemporary supporters of the Noble Lie. He knew that he was but the last link in a long chain of those who had fought against the inculcation of superstition for reasons of state."

But our concern with Lucretius is not historical, so much as analytical. In this too, Lucretius offers clear indications that his view of mind and society is the direct opposite of Platonic idealism, as expressed in the allegory of the cave. "This dread and darkness of the mind cannot be dispelled by the sunbeams, the shining shafts of day, but only by an understanding of the outward form and inner workings of nature." Lucretius follows this statement of a naturalistic view with the claim that "Nothing can ever be created by divine power out of nothing. The reason why all mortals are so gripped by fear is that they see all sorts of things happening on the earth and in the sky with no discernible cause, and these they attribute to the will of a god." (Cf. Lucretius, 1951:31.) The reason for distortions of truth, for Lucretius, is not that men dwell in caves of darkness, but that the knowledge men possess is so severely limited in predictive potential, that false extensions are made from our present knowledge.

The Epicureans distinguished between that which we know factually and that which the mind demands absolute answers to despite the limits of knowledge. It is the quest for certainty that accounts for false beliefs, not the social origins of ordinary men. Like Hsün-Tzu, Lucretius noted that men were at a loss to account for cosmological happenings, so· thus "took refuge in handing over everything to the gods and making everything dependent on their whim. They chose the sky to be the home and headquarters of the gods because it is through the sky that the moon is seen to tread its cyclic course with day and night, and night's ominous constellations and the night-flying torches and soaring flames of the firmament, clouds and sun and rain, snow and wind, lightning and hail, the sudden thunder-crash and the long-drawn intimidating rumble." (*Ibid.*, 1951:207.)

Ignorance of the laws of nature creates the seeds for mystifying the unkown. Far from preserving truth from the hordes of ignorant masses, the Platonic myth-maker spends most of his time strangulating truth in convincing men of the naturalness of aristocratic domination. "Poor humanity," Lucretius moans, "to saddle the gods with such responsibilities and throw in a vindictive temper! What griefs they hatched then for themselves, what festering sores for us, what tears for our posterity." (*Ibid.*, 1951: 208.) Religion, far from necessarily preserving order as Plato held, is the epitome of false consciousness, and therefore of the ills plaguing men. The fusion of social order and intellectual deceit is, for Lucretius, the seed-bed of revolution.

The conflict between these mighty ancients was complete. But both operated in a universe of discourse quite new to mankind— society. Thus, whatever the actual relation between material reality and ideal forms, between the leaders and the led, the distinction between these phenomena represented a new stage in philosophic evolution. Both took for granted that knowledge is a product of man's social life; and on this account that men are not only distinguished from the rest of nature, but more significantly, from each other. The conflict in ideas and ideals was thus related to the contrasting roles of men as social and political creatures.

BACON AND HUME

Francis Bacon was responsible for major landmarks in the prehistory of the sociology of knowledge on two counts. He developed the first typology of the sources of distortion in human understanding; and he also attempted a social explanation of philosophical errors. These interconnected points remain firm guides to those sociologists of knowledge anchored to an empirical appraisal of ideas.

Bacon was led to his social interpretations of epistemology through a belief that "the human understanding is no dry light, but receives an infusion from the will and affections. For what a man had rather were true he more readily believes." Because of this, the man of knowledge, who is no less the man of interests, "rejects difficult things from impatience of research; sober things, because they narrow hope; the deeper things of nature, from superstition; the light of experience, from arrogance and pride, lest his mind should seem to be occupied with things mean and transitory; things not commonly believed, out of deference to the opinion of the vulgar. Numberless in short are the ways, and sometimes imperceptible, in which the affections colour and infect the understanding." (Bacon, 1620:xlix.)

In his characterization of the four types of false consciousness in philosophy, Bacon advanced a distinctly sociological thesis. In fact, although the terms "idol" and "ideology" bear only a superficial linguistic resemblance, the latter term not coming into use until the nineteenth century writings of Destutt de Tracy and Karl Marx, Bacon leaves no doubt that he is using idol not so much in the religious sense of pagan worship, but rather as a synonym for socially conditioned faulty reasoning.

In the first idol Bacon denounces, we have an example of his efforts at an anthropomorphic reorientation of philosophy. The idols of the Tribe, the notions built about the premise that man is the measure of things, rest primarily on Bacon's belief that this idol is rooted in man as a self-protective social animal. He sees anthropomorphic tribal attitudes to knowledge as a "false mirror" which, "receiving rays irregularly, distorts and discolors the nature of things by mingling its own nature with it." He then points to the fact that while the social preoccupations of men inform the affections and the will, they no less deform the senses. The idol remains powerful because it is a reinforcement of the quest for security in what is imagined to be a precarious, contingent world. (*Ibid.*, xli, lii.)

The remaining three idols reveal Bacon's tendency to equate varied types of false understanding with specific characteristics of the contending social forces of seventeenth century English life: the politically dominant aristocracy, the urban centered commercial interests, the only extant professional intelligentsia—the high clergy.

The idols of the Cave, of the individual rather than of social man, exhibits that narrowness and provinciality characteristic of the learned, humanist-oriented aristocracy. They are errors which arise "owing either to his own proper and peculiar nature or to his education and conversation with others; or to the reading of books, and the authority of those whom he esteems and admires." These are in sum, the idols of men who search for science in their own private worlds of discourse, and not in the greater world of nature. (*Ibid.*, xlii, liii.) The idols of the Market-Place are more distinctly business-like in character, since they are formed in the "commerce and consort of men," and in either a real or synthetic market-place. This group fetishizes words as they deify the functions of the economic system of exchange. They throw everything into a confusion in which the idols of words overcome the proper comprehension of reality. (*Ibid.*, xliii, lx.) The idol of the Theater, the false notions absorbed from philosophic rivalries inherited from a hoary past, is the Achilles' heel of the intellectual clergy. The belief in received systems, which Bacon considers "so many stage plays," represents the world in an unreal and detached fashion. Bacon pauses to point out that these idols are not innate or secretive, a clear reference to the Scholastics, but arise in everyone infected by this particular idol, through literary, philosophic and theologic falsehoods, informed by a "false logic." Bacon closes his critique of the idols of the Theater with a reminder that "when a man runs the wrong way, the more active and swift he is the further he will go astray." (*Ibid.*, xliv.)

While Farrington (1949) and Zilsel (1942) may have interpolated a stricter correlation of consciousness and class than Bacon was perhaps aware of, it is hard to see what other interpretation can be placed on his theory and criticism of the idols. What Bacon offers is clearly not a *philosophical* reply to what may be considered epistemological errors; he even opens his *Organum* by declaring the hopelessness of such an approach. What he does present is a *sociological* critique of the philosophic conscience gone wrong.

This modern aspect of Bacon's work should not, however, lead us too far afield. Attempts to place Bacon at the start of the empirical tradition, overlook his immersion in Greek and Medieval rationalism. (Cf. Anderson, 1948.) The efforts to make him into a pure naturalist ignore his inclusion of empiricism, along with sophistry and superstition, among the parent stock of errors. Bacon was, as a matter of conviction, supremely confident in the rational order of nature and mind alike. As such, he never questioned the possibility of reaching the absolute truth; although the method of getting knowledge was for him experimental and not rationalistic. Rationalism is converted into True Philosophy or Science. What limits Bacon's sociological sense is, why, if the idols he so trenchantly describes, are useful to its entrenched holders, need they be overcome? This issue never arose since Bacon never questioned the capacity of the rational faculties to overcome superstition and the ability of all men in common to arrive at a true interpretation of nature.

In the larger issues of philosophy, Bacon exhibited rare foresight. He escaped extreme relativism, not by declaring in favor of the truth potential of a single social class or intellectual elite, but by his optimistic faith in the truth making and truth breaking potential of a technological vitalization of society. The capacity of science to disclose "the mind not only in its own faculties, but in its connection with things, must needs hold that the art of discovery may advance as discoveries advance." (Bacon, 1620:cxxx.) In present-day terms, Bacon's contribution inhered in the socially verified belief that the question of truth is solved in the practice and progress of an industrial way of life.

What Bacon's analysis of the idols meant for the revitalization of a general theory of science, David Hume's criticism of idolatry signified as a new empirical look at religious experience. The basis of empiricist thought is not so much the difference between what we sense and what we think we sense as it is a distinction between what we *perceive* and what we *conceive*. This distinction between percept and concept is turned to religious concerns by Hume in his essay, *The Natural History of Religion* (1757). Root (1956) regards this study as the beginning of the philosophy of religion. Whether this is so or not, there is no gainsaying that Hume's critique of idolatry carried the Baconian vision to unexplored heights.

Hume's approach to idolatry, while not as clearly structured as Bacon's consideration of idols, can nonetheless, be subdivided into the consideration of four distinct conceptual types.

The first reason for idolatry, and perhaps the most important for Hume, is ignorance; specifically, ignorance of causation. "Mankind, being placed in such an absolute ignorance of causes, and being at the same time so anxious concerning their future fortune, should immediately acknowledge a dependence on invisible powers, possessed of sentiment and intelligence." (Hume, 1757: 30.) The cycle is from ignorance to exaggeration of the unknown, to the eventual deification of what we are ignorant. Hume closes his study by giving as a maxim: "ignorance is the mother of devotion."

Ignorance, however, is not yet idolatry. It is but the conversion of the unknown into concrete images that allows for idolatry. "The vulgar polytheist, so far from admitting that idea, deifies every part of the universe, and conceives all the conspicuous productions of nature, to be themselves so many real divinities. The sun, moon and stars are all gods according to his system: Fountains are inhabited by nymphs, and trees by hamadryads. Even monkeys, dogs, cats, and other animals often become sacred in his eyes, and strike him with a religious veneration. And thus, however strong men's propensity to believe invisible, intelligent power in nature, their propensity is equally strong to rest their attention on sensible, visible objects; and in order to reconcile these opposite inclinations, they are led to unite the invisible power with some visible object." (*Ibid.*, 38.)

The second cause for idolatry is absolute power, the transformation of the ordinary man who has political power into an object of admiration. Here Hume offers the first formulation of Weber's concept of charismatic personality. "When every strain of flattery has been exhausted towards arbitrary princes, when every human quality has been applauded to the utmost; their servile courtiers represent them, at last, as real divinities, and point them out to the people as objects of adoration." (*Ibid.*, 43.) The further abstraction of humanized power is divinized power. The leader is alternatively flattered, praised, eulogized, and his virtues exaggerated. The quantity and quality of adulation varies in direct proportion to the absoluteness of political power. Hume's sense of the social was not, however, as precise, as Bacon's. Hume had an aristocratic tendency to connect the vulgar mass with polytheistic forms of worship and the intellectually sophisticated with theism. But this connection has its limitations since Hume does point out that there is a historical "flux and reflux" from idolatry to theism and then back again to more primitive forms of belief. Indeed, Hume tends to associate despotic power with monotheism and tolerance with polytheism. "Idolatry is attended with this evident advantage, that, by limiting the powers and functions of its deities, it naturally admits the gods of other sects and nations to a share of divinity, and renders all the various deities, as well as rites, ceremonies, or traditions, compatible with each other." (*Ibid.*, 48.)

The third major cornerstone of idolatry is fear. Hume might well have had in mind the example of the English *virtuosi*, who, the more convinced they were of the accuracy of Newton's mechanistic physics, the more desperate in defense of orthodox Anglicanism they became. Thus such major scientific minds of the age as Bentley, Boyle, Glanville and Charleton spent most of their time arguing against the non-existent threat of atheism. (Cf. Westfall, 1958.) Here Hume's penetrating psychological insight leads him to note that the more factual information falling into the hands of the religious enthusiast the more superstitious does he become. Empirical evidence does not shake his dogmatism, the enthusiast only convinces himself further of the need for belief.

The idolatrous results of fear are the product of an intensification of differences between formal, ritualist religions and genuinely felt convictions. "Notwithstanding the dogmatical, imperious style of all superstition, the conviction of the religionists in all ages is more affected than real, and scarcely ever approaches, in any degree, to that solid belief and persuasion, which governs us in the common affairs of life." In conclusion, Hume observes that "men dare not avow, even to their own hearts, the doubts which they entertain on such subjects. They make a merit of implicit faith; and disguise to themselves their real infidelity, by the strongest asseverations and most positive bigotry." (*Ibid.*, 60.)

The fourth cause for idolatry is that elusive factor which the Enlightenment felt was diametrically opposed to religious pietism —the quest for happiness. For Hume, happiness, no less than ignorance, fear or power, leads to exaggeration and to a deification of nature. This takes place since happiness, like the other passions, is a cause of anxiety. "The active imagination of men, uneasy in this abstract conception of objects, about which it is incessantly employed, begins to render them more particular, and to clothe them in shapes more suitable to its natural comprehension. It represents them (the deities—ILH) to be sensible, intelligent beings, like mankind; actuated by love and hatred, and flexible by gifts and entreaties, by prayers and sacrifices. Hence the origin of a religion." (*Ibid.*, 47.) The unrealistic, anxious concern for happiness thus promotes a distortion of reality and results in error.

These then are the four causes of idolatry. Like Bacon, Hume had no interest in destroying religion, only in showing that "the first religious principles must be secondary." The importance of Bacon and Hume for the development of a sociology of knowledge inheres in their unique capacity to distinguish between the thoughts and deeds of men. As Hume puts it: "Hear the verbal protestations of all men: Nothing so certain as their religious tenets. Examine their lives: You will scarcely think that they repose the smallest confidence in them. The greatest and truest zeal gives us no security against hypocrisy: The most open impiety is attended with a secret dread and compunction." (*Ibid.*, 75.)

English empiricism was both the historical and phenomenological precondition for eighteenth century Encyclopedism to develop a fuller theory of the social roots of the distortion of truth. And men like Voltaire, Condillac and Helvetius made no secret of this intellectual debt.

MALEBRANCHE AND HELVETIUS

Considering the fact that Nicolas Malebranche wrote no work on social philosophy, it might seem rather strange that he has come to be considered a parent to the sociology of knowledge. (Cf. Speier, 1952.) This reputation is, nonetheless, deserved. It is derived from his phenomenological description of how different people act and think according to the different occupations and interests they have. This is the main point of Malebranche's masterful *Recherche de la Verité* (1674-75).

The study of nature, no less than the study of geometry, morals and theology, reveals eternal and immutable truths that are identical to an almighty and uncreated God. Malebranche offered this in opposition to sensualist philosophies which believed that stable moral rules could be directly gotten from a knowledge of physical principles. Descartes had already distinguished between intellect and body, *res cogitans* and *res extensa*. Only the former was held to have the capacity of locating truth; the senses, as an extension of the body were properly subject to the laws of the mind. Human understanding, when applied to physics and mathematics is itself simply God's *logos* or *Verbum* brought to bear on natural events.

Malebranche recognized two faculties of the soul: the understanding and the inclination. The first receives ideas, while the second digests them. He follows Descartes in thinking that no change occurs in the soul which is not accompanied by bodily variation: there is no understanding without images absorbed from the senses, and there is no inclination without passion. Now while everyone has the same understanding and inclination, there remain wide differences in sensations and passions among different individuals. Malebranche attributes these differences to original sin, which severed the harmonious relation of body and soul. But the psychological working out of such differences in sensations and passions is offered by him as logical truisms.

In *Recherche de la Verité*, five of the six sections are dedicated to locating the sources of error in the senses, imagination, understanding, inclinations, and the passions. The method Malebranche uses is deductive and rationalistic; the examples were individualistic, i.e., a phenomenological description of individual differences that can be found among the different types of people in any given society.

The psychological relativism of Malebranche is best presented in the following passage, in which it will be seen that his line of reasoning stands quite independent of theological proofs. "The difference observable in Men, as to their Ways and Purposes in Life, are almost infinite. Their different conditions, different Employments, different Posts and Offices and different Communities are innumerable. These Differences are the Reason of Man's acting upon quite different Designs; and Reasoning upon different principles. Even in the same Community, wherein there should be but one Character of Mind, and all the same Designs; you shall rarely meet with several Persons, whose aims and views are not different." Malebranche concludes by noting that "their various Employments and their many adhesions necessarily diversify the Method and Manner they would take to accomplish those very things wherein they agree." (*Ibid.*, 75.)

Malebranche had a remarkable capacity to distinguish overt from hidden motives. The springs of human action stem from the latter and are rationalized later. To be sure, he was always the philosopher: pointing out ways of combatting hidden motives when we must, and turning them to purposeful account when possible. As Levy-Bruhl (1899) indicated, "he had a most delicate psychological sense, and his clear-sightedness may even occasionally be merciless."

In the sense that the eighteenth century *philosophe*, Claude Helvetius, had as his chief concern the relation between motivation and action, he was a direct descendant of Descartes and Malebranche. *De l'Esprit* (1758) the only work published during Helvetius' lifetime, deals primarily with the problem of the sources of error and false judgments. These are directly caused by human passions and ignorance. The passions, e.g., luxury, pride, impatience, allow us to see only one side of things. We thus arrive at a point where all experience is judged in terms of this one side. Our ideas, maintains Helvetius, cannot reach perfection if the process of acquiring them is blocked by the passions or ruled over by ignorance.

The factors, which for Helvetius lead to a distortion of knowledge, might be placed in the form of a paradigm. (a) What we term *personal* passions: pride, ambitions, impatience, operate on an individual psychological level as factors of error. (b) The *social* passions: such as ambition, luxury and ostentation. These passions, operating on politics and economics, have to be viewed primarily in terms of their social consequences. (c) *Epistemological* distortions, which consists primarily in the misuse and abuse of language, and of confused ideas attached to ordinary language. Helvetius reproduces Locke's analysis of matter. He does not delve deeply into distortions in our knowledge due to issues of perception and conception. Helvetius was convinced that Locke had completed the task of resolving this third type of error.

Helvetius' contributions to social thought is thus greater than his work in philosophy as such. He explicitly placed the factors of error and false judgment at a sociological level. What these factors are specifically is a task he addressed himself to. To begin with, all new ideas were held to stem from physical sensibility and memory, the latter being dependent on the former, memory being but an extension of thought in general. By distinguishing perception (psychological) from judgment (social), Helvetius showed the possibility of there being different kinds of mistakes.

In the Second Discourse of *De l'Esprit,* Helvetius deals with the relation between Mind and Society. Here he examines the question of why men consider and judge different actions and ideas in terms of self-interest. Judgments, asserts Helvetius, depend upon interests. We call actions and ideas virtuous when they are useful to us, vicious when they harm us, worthless when their consequences are trivial for us. The hedonistic calculus is thus turned upon the foundations of knowledge itself.

Helvetius offers a classification of interests in terms of whom they effect: particular, specific individuals; small groups and institutions, such as factories, the church, professional societies; national interests; the temporal and spatial interests of different epochs and civilizations; universal interests, such as norms for behaviour that would guarantee the continuation of the human race. Thus interests of men involve a gamut of considerations that enable individual interests to harmonize with universal interests automatically, much in the manner of a laisser-faire economic system.

We have seen that for Helvetius, actions and ideas are virtuous when self-interest can be connected up to social interests. However, judgments as to interests, might easily be distorted. Thus Helvetius finds it necessary to distinguish between prejudiced virtues and true virtues, that is, between actions that allow or disallow for the public happiness. Political corruption and religious intolerance are thus considered vested interests that disturb the proper functioning of a commonwealth—happiness of the individual. Society and its interests must therefore submit to the will of the individual, since only the latter can, properly speaking, be a bearer of truth.

Unlike Malebranche, Helvetius recognized that nature has distributed talent in unequal proportions. There are people with more "esprit" (understanding for Malebranche) than others. But every rational creature has at least the minimum of "esprit" to reach the highest ideals. Our passions propel the human spirit farther, overcoming the petty self-interests along the way, and in so doing, eliminating obstacles to a proper understanding of society. Equality is desired rather than assumed to be the condition of man. It is a want rather than a fact. Only education can convert this moral desire into actuality. The purpose of De l'Homme (1772) is to develop this point that instruction and education are decisive in the formation of a human personality. If legislation has functioned to promote selfish interests, then it is the job of education to overcome legislation, to transcend politics, and promote the public interest, the mass interests. The possibility that knowledge might serve selfish interests just as ably as public interests apparently was never entertained by Helvetius. He was too much the man of Enlightenment to envision a situation in which true knowledge could function without regard to values of social happiness and popular consensus.

Helvetius' work rests on the hidden premise that self and society are ultimately harmonious; and that the true passions of the former are convertible into the currency of the latter. Helvetius illustrates the Encyclopedic temper of mind to consider all things as phenomenally available for inspection. Thus, passions, interests and needs all operate at the same level of society. The moment German romantic rationalism announced a division between phenomenal and noumenal events, between knowledge of appearance and reality, indeed, between forms of knowledge itself, the psychological insights into the working of society provided by French eighteenth century philosophy became for Kant and Hegel but a moment in the all-inclusive, cosmological re-orientation of the place of mind in the social order.

KANT, HEGEL AND FEUERBACH

An accurate gauge of the importance of the work of Kant, Hegel and Feuerbach for the development of a sociology of knowledge is hardly possible. Their work has been so thoroughly absorbed into the mainstream of social thought that we must content ourselves with a brief introduction to the main outlines. It will be seen that the issues raised by these three philosophers of early nineteenth century Germany remain central in present discussions of the content of a sociological approach to knowledge.

Immanuel Kant's contribution to the formation of a sociology of knowledge stemmed from his rejection of the phenomenalist-empiricist epistemology. In contradistinction to the empiricism of Bacon, Locke and Hume, and no less, the sensationalism of Helvetius and Condillac, Kant, in his *Critique of Pure Reason* (1781) asserted that knowledge is basically a consequence of the mental life of man, rather than a series of experienced events. But in addition, knowledge is more than thinking. It is made possible by the apriori constructions of consciousness. "I do not know any object by merely thinking, but only by determining a given intuition with respect to that unity of consciousness in which all thought consists." (Bk. II, ch. 1.)

Science, knowledge—the terms are equivalent for Kant—does not exist without definite metaphysical presuppositions about the structure and texture of reality. Man starts with clear-cut commitments about knowledge possessed without having tested (or even the need to test) these commitments by pure empirical methods. We begin with a categorical apparatus for establishing truths; a categorical system which services knowledge of morals and religion no less than knowledge of mathematics and physics. Thus the truths we have of the former are no less certain than the truths possessed of the latter.

Philosophically, Kant attempted to mediate the distinction between nature and mind. He declared "the existence of all objects of the external senses to be doubtful. This uncertainty I call the ideality of external phenomena, and the doctrine of that ideality is called idealism; in comparison with which the other doctrine, which maintains a possible certainty of the objects of the external senses is called dualism." (Bk. II, ch. 1.) This comment, labeled by Kant the "fourth paralogism of ideality" has its rough equivalent in Max Weber's "ideal type." For both Kant and Weber, the laws posited of external nature are *considered* real on conventionalist grounds, and not on empirically based information. The paralogisms of Kant enabled him to establish a theory of knowledge that in principle would not be subject to the caprice of metaphysical presuppositions. As part of the categorical system, the paralogisms could be distinguished from social ideologies in that the former are fixed, universal and the property of pure reason itself.

If the phenomenal world shows reason itself to be grounded in all sorts of private interests and attitudes, this only demonstrated for Kant the inadequacy of phenomenalist explanations, and not the shortcomings of reason. In the form of the intellectual, the worker, the professional, this distinction between the bearer of reason and the bearer of interests, has been reproduced many times over in the sociology of knowledge; always with the subtle Kantian belief that knowledge is something over and above the empirical world which verifies its existence.

Kant attempted to establish a doctrine of knowledge upon transcendentally revealed principles. Hegel reversed this position by bringing the transcendent back into the historical flow, that is, by making knowledge subject to the laws of change rather than to the laws of formal logic. (Cf. Marcuse, 1941: ch. 7.)

We can range Hegel's contributions to the pre-history of the sociology of knowledge into five phases, each of which were necessary for the development of a theory of ideology and of the social genesis of religion, law, ethics, science, and philosophy itself. To begin with, Hegel, in his *Science of Logic* (1812) liquified the Kantian categories, making them a moment in time. This unusual work, which might just as easily be entitled the *Science of Metaphysics,* further attempted to reveal the ontological status of logical form. Once a logic *with* ontology is accepted, it is clear that Kant, who took the Aristotelian logic at face value (Kant's set of antinomies were held to exist at a pragmatic level rather than a logical level), was faced with the ineluctable dilemma of showing where and how pure reason could be both separate and identical with the flux of reality. For Hegel, truth is real, independent of perception, as it is rational. But that is only because history, the living history of stones, plants, animals and people, is real and rational.

The initial stage in Hegel's architectonic was evolved in the *Phenomenology of Mind* (1807). This work is a gigantic attempt to show that the development of human reason is coincidental with the historical evolution of nature and society. This is no effort at a chronological history of theories of mind, but rather an attempt to unfold the logical stages by which and through which the mind reaches its present level of understanding. From the observation of brute matter to the formation of laws of thought, Hegel takes us through the painstaking effort of the human spirit to continually synthesize present and past dilemmas (called contradictions). The phenomenological evolution of thought is thus itself part of the historical world. This evolutionary process ends for Hegel with reason identifying itself with reason as such, stripped of the contradictions and vagaries present in history in general and in the history of thought in particular.

In his final authenticated work, *Philosophy of Right and Law* (1820), Hegel produced the social capstone to his general theory of knowledge as historical. Knowledge becomes a socially viable instrument only when transformed into the concrete, into law, ethics and philosophy. The canonization of ideas, their use for specific social goals by specific social and economic classes, whether it be the legal basis of marriage or the military basis of the State, reveals knowledge no longer as purely rational. The function of ideas in concrete life is not bound by a categorical imperative, but by categorical interests. But these interests are not chosen interests, or interests held in human consciousness as the French Enlightenment thought and taught. The opposite is the case. The real interests of men are veiled in the anonymity of social history. Thus the true interests of men are different from those which they themselves proclaim. (Hegel, 1820: preface.)

Two posthumously published volumes, derived from lecture notes, also deserve mention in that they help fill in the content of the Hegelian system. *The Philosophy of History* (1837) is an attempt to impart meaning to the dialectical transformations of societies and civilizations. No longer concerned with the operations of a single social system, Hegel is able to give a classification of social changes that has as its purpose the identification of human purpose with the unconscious motor forces of history. In this way, the relativity of an individual, or of a particular society, can be considered an unconditioned absolute, i.e., as an absolute stage in the unfolding of objective consciousness, or better, in the process of history.

Hegel's *Lectures on the History of Philosophy* (1833-36) offers a final clue for understanding latter-day sociologists of knowledge like Karl Mannheim and Alfred Weber. For if the true interests of men differ from supposed interests, if objective consciousness is distinct from private egoistic consciousness, it is clear that some group of men might be able to distinguish the two. Here the philosopher enters the historical scene. He is charged with the momentous task of separating science and appearance, true consciousness and false consciousness. "When the history of Philosophy has to tell of deeds in history, we first ask, what a deed in Philosophy is; and whether any particular thing is philosophic or not. In external history everything is in action—certainly there is in it what is important and that which is unimportant—but action is the idea immediately placed before us. This is not the case in Philosophy, and on this account the history of Philosophy cannot be treated throughout without the introduction of the historian's view." (1833-36:116.) The fusion of the historian's moment and the philosopher's sense of the transcendent is thus the essential way into Truth and Reason.

Ludwig Feuerbach, the philosopher who materialized the Hegelian consciousness, is neither as seminal a mind as his predecessor, nor as original as the critic of Hegel's idealism, Marx, and the critic of Hegel's historicism, Nietzsche. Nevertheless, Feuerbach made a profound contribution to the origins of the sociology of knowledge through his "unmasking" of the religious consciousness.

Feuerbach was the first great pioneer in the social study of religion as distinct from German Higher Biblical criticism carried on by Lessing, Jacobi and Mendelssohn. He noted that the problem of the truth content of religious doctrines is quite apart from the social genesis of religion as such. Further, Feuerbach distinguished between the religious impulses, "true religion," and the rationalization of these impulses, "theology." In his famous work, *The Essence of Christianity* (1841), it is noted that: "The true sense of Theology is Anthropology, that there is no distinction between the predicates of the diverse and human nature, and, consequently, no distinction between the divine and human subject" (ch. 1).

A special achievement registered by Feuerbach was to show religion, not as the French Enlightenment did, as simple false consciousness; but more profoundly, as a distorted aspect of true consciousness. "The *truth*, the *essence* of religion, is that it conceives and affirms a profoundly human relation as a divine relation." Whereas Voltaire offered a *chronique scandaleuse*, Feuerbach attempted to provide the study of religion, particularly Christianity, with a distinctively sociological setting. It was a view of religion as an object of history rather than as a subject for exposé. Feuerbach was therefore led to conceive of "anthropological philosophy" not exclusively or even primarily as ideological unmasking, but as a positive social science.

The reason we can justifiably end the "pre-history" of the sociology of knowledge with Feuerbach, is that despite his in-

ability to escape the content and vocabulary of Christianity—
something Karl Barth well notes (1926:212-39)—he was the first
to announce the impotence of philosophy to treat religion objectively. The reason for this is that philosophy taken as metaphysics
is itself a form of religious consciousness, and as such contributes
to the estrangement of man from his social environment. This
scuttling of metaphysics, combined with Feuerbach's conversion
of materialism into social science, is called by Marx the "great
achievement" of Feuerbach (1844:145). And properly understood, it is just that. For from this time on, philosophy, like religion, morals and law, became open to sociological study. The
iron-clad separation of the sacred and the profane was broken by
the force of "true materialism," that is, anthropology and sociology.

Chapter III

Empirical Description and
Social Prescriptions

THE history of the sociology of knowledge is a history of the shedding of its metaphysical inheritance. Philosophy, which in its primitive stages covered the gamut of natural and social history, at present has given way to the sciences. The velocity and rate of acceleration of this transformation of philosophy into science can be measured by the fact that as late as the nineteenth century, physics was still considered part of natural philosophy.

Science, the discovery, verification and explanation of objective laws, has had to engage in a steady polemic against the claims of transcendental and intuitionist philosophies alike. The results of this dialogue, however, are no longer conjectural. With Galileo and Newton, physics became separated from metaphysics. And as Philipp Frank (1952) adds: "Mechanics, physics, chemistry, in fact all branches of knowledge underwent a similar division (to geometrical astronomy) as they developed to the point where observable facts could be derived from abstract principles through the logic of mathematics." Next, with Darwin and Wallace, biology separated itself from generalized, teleological descriptions and classifications of plant and animal life, formerly labeled the philosophy of nature. Later in the nineteenth century, with Freud and Pavlov, psychology declared its independence from epistemology, thereby completing the basic methodological re-orientation of scientific thought.

The germs of this separation of science from philosophy are hardly recent. They can be found in Aristotle, the philosopher most responsible for the classification of the sciences as an extension of philosophy. The Stagirite, in providing the basic generic and genetic distinctions in levels of abstract thought, in effect, pointed the way towards the liberation of empirical research from deductive rationalization, just as he himself sought to separate the philosophical from the magical. The next major step was undertaken by Kant, who clearly stated that the observable facts of the physical world are completely and satisfactorily described and systematized by science proper. Thus at the level of phenomenal events, science is a complete system. Kant did this not to liquidate philosophy, but to save it by removing it to a realm beyond the field of experience. Once this division between science and philosophy became firmly implanted, it opened up all kinds of interpretations as to the meaning of philosophy—a search for perennial values, the urge of reason to attain a synthetic vision, a logical handmaiden to the sciences—but it actually achieved the more important task of freeing empirical sciences from their common metaphysical, Platonic inheritance.

This is no place to offer a prognosis as to the future of philosophy. It might be pointed out however, that its ancient function of critical judgment is enhanced rather than impaired by the rise of science. Philosophy rests on rational rather than empirical grounds. It makes no discoveries in the scientific sense because it provides no laws, no statements of explanation for the purpose of predicting future events. In its analytic capacities, philosophy is therefore rational in the logical sense that mathematics is rational. Both provide formal, logical criteria applicable to a wide range of problems generated by social living and scientific needs.

The twentieth century has continued the reformation of philosophy, albeit a reformation going on in spite of, rather than as a consequence of philosophical literature. Epistemology has disintegrated as the ultimate preserve of philosophy. In the nineteenth century, the theory of knowledge in its physical and biological aspects was taken over by the science of psychology. In the twentieth century, epistemology in its social aspects has moved beyond the social metaphysics of Comte and Spencer and now functions as the sociology of knowledge. The environmental side of epistemology has given way to the empirical study of the social and cultural determinants of knowledge. How these determinants and their deviants help form the content and contours of human ideas is the essential field of the sociology of knowledge.

Each new science first uses the language of the common philosophic ancestor of all the sciences. This was no less true of physics in the hands of Kepler, than it is of the sociology of knowledge in the hands of Mannheim. This may at times prove misleading, to the degree that casting new ideas in traditional philosophic language, tends to disguise genuine discoveries of science.

Even prior to the work of Mannheim and Scheler, the two men usually associated with the discovery of the sociology of knowledge, Durkheim and Weber worked tirelessly to remove archaic, inherited phraseology from social science in favor of a more suitable vocabulary. The growth of a science involves an ever deepening immersion in concrete problems. The process of separating science and metaphysics is not mechanical, not a result of slogans and myths, but an enterprise involving a great deal of positively expended energy to define the boundaries of a new science and then to explore in detail the contents of these boundaries.

The sociology of knowledge comes into existence only at that time when knowledge is understood as a dynamic social force in its own right; and at a period in human affairs when knowledge is viewed as a central agency in social change. This discipline is not simply a theory of European philosophers. The investigations by Fried (1942) and Laswell (1946) into the relation of propaganda and public opinions; by Berelson (1951) on content analysis in communications; by Merton (1957; Pt. II, ch. vii) on the role of intellectuals in bureaucratic structures; and by Lazarsfeld (1955) on mass communications generally, all indicate that the earlier statements of Weber, Mannheim and Scheler were essentially correct. Knowledge, however we define that word, can be studied directly since it produces direct, combustible political consequences.

The sociology of knowledge investigates the ideational factors compelling men to act, not the moral propriety of such action. The moral implications of modern physics are properly the *social* concern of physicists. To ask of the physicist that he should sub-

mit his experimental research to politically sanctioned value judgments is to undermine the empirical basis of physics itself. Likewise, the sociology of knowledge is not part of a general moral
system. It may study the functioning of morals in socially fluid
situations, and in the thought formations that enter into the
creation of these situations, but it does not rest on the standpoint
of a moral code or political credo as such.

This is not to say that the sociology of knowledge eschews a
moral purpose. It is, as Dilthey (V:317, VII:63-4) noted, committed to social progress precisely through its capacity to logically
distinguish moral-theological theories from empirical assertions.

Weber (1924) carried the theory of a *wertfrei Wissenschaft*
a step further by noting that "once one has acknowledged the
logical disjunction between the two spheres, it seems to me that
the assumption of this attitude (of a genuinely ethical attitude)
is an imperative requirement of intellectual honesty; in this case,
it is the absolutely minimal requirement." Unlike some of his
more ardent followers, however, Weber had the good sense not to
erect a philosophical dualism out of a simple logical disjunction.

The empirical foundations of the sociology of knowledge inhere
in the discovery that science is distinct from ideology, that representation in consciousness of laws of nature or society involves a
different approach to the treatment of raw information than the
practical consciousness impregnated with regional, class or national interests. Nonetheless, this distinction is no barrier to investigation of the social sources and condition of science as well
as of ideology. The discovery of types of knowledge, and the
various social uses for each type, determines the content and
limits of the sociology of knowledge.

The content of the sociology of knowledge can be selectively
summarized at this point to mean the following: (a) the empirical
study of the ways ideas are used to galvanize action; (b) the
social basis of ideas, irrespective of their truth or falsity; (c) the
ideational conditions for the survival of social motivation; (d)
the use of ideas and values to promote new forms of social relations, and the use of counter-ideas and counter-values to frustrate
new forms; (e) the respective functions of science, religion, myth
and logic in the creation of ideological conceptions of the uni-

verse; (f) the treatment of knowledge as an independent variable with its unique dynamics of change.

Such a summary clearly takes for granted the values of science. As Wolff (1943) has stated, instead of asserting the priority of this or that form of social action, the sociology of knowledge inquires into the nature and legitimacy of assumed priorities. Take for example, the notion that man thinks with blood rather than with brains. This implies a commitment to an ideology and to a kind of action grounded in irrationality. However, if one seeks the causal ground for the promulgation and acceptance of such notions as racial stocks, or their political consequences, then the very idea of thinking with blood is undermined in the act of rational, scientific investigation.

A rational description of ideologies is suspect to those who employ ideologies for special-interest ends, even supposedly beneficient ends. For as early as Marx (1859), it was known that the nature of an ideology requires unquestioning allegiance, conscious or unconscious. If a doctor presents a patient with a prescription and asserts that such and such a dose will cure the illness, we usually follow the prescription. We do so because were we to inquire into why such a prescription will yield the anticipated results, or whether other illnesses might not be consequent from the prescription, our empirical query would be answered. What distinguishes the modern physician from the tribal medicine man is the willingness in principle of the former to submit his prescription to critical scrutiny. Because of its invasion of the territory of conventional dogma, the sociology of knowledge has become the newest of the "dangerous sciences." Unexamined, untested, social prescriptions are too frequently not the cure, but the disease. They offer action to be sure, but of such a nature as to be divorced from anticipated consequences. Sorel (1908) realized that to some extent this division between the two derives from a conventionalist theory of science. But this does not give anyone the right to assume a *necessary* dualism between theory and what is being theorized about. To do so, would convert the sociology of knowledge from a dangerous science into a dismal science.

The sociology of knowledge employs a series of variables which operate on several levels. Whether these levels are monistically or pluralistically conceived is not at issue. What is significant is that cognizance of their existence, and consequently their use in the actual work of the sociology of knowledge, precede the resolution of "ultimate" questions. As Simmel indicated (1908), to start with so-called ultimate questions is to transform social science into social theology. The ultimate question is the irrational question; and the irrational question is the unscientific question.

The range of variables employed by the sociology of knowledge commences with the biological, social and cultural foundations in which men find themselves at a given time. The integration of various levels of life is a cardinal way of providing operational criteria. Only transcendental metaphysics offers an analysis of Man and Society apart from men in societies. Behaviour is concrete, functioning in terms of situations and relations men are involved in. We need not accept the non-intellective theories of Parsons to see the wisdom in his idea that behaviour is both "a function of the relation of the actor to his situation and the history of that relation" (1951a).

For the sociology of knowledge, the central core of its studies are the attitudes, motives and orientations employed to justify the defense or critique of existing social relations, and the activity generated by such attitudes. Distinguishing this level of social reality, it might be noted that each individual has a unique operational base and accordingly forms a special image of this base. Such involvements offer an opportunity to study the relation between involvement and distortions of thought. The circulation of political elites, psychological taboos, mass revolutions, as well as more intimate details of family and community structure, offer fertile ground for the analysis of the inter-connection of social mobility and ideologies. (Cf. Childe, 1949.)

The symbols and myths which individuals and groups adopt to fulfill the requirements of political prophecy, no less than social change, is a primary element in the formation of ideology and counter-ideology. The sociology of knowledge must understand the social group to which symbols and imagery are conveyed, and in addition, the responses to such symbolization. The study of consensus in small groups entails a recognition that truth-making is distinct from truth-seeking, and that myth-making differs from myth-following. It is evident that action is made and stimulated at various levels; not the least of which is the objective calculation of the stimuli value of a symbol. This effort to rationalize the irrational play of forces in society reached its high-point in Pareto's (1916) inclusive system of social statics. Here the irrational urge to political power is taken for granted, while the apparatus of power, elites, myths, slogans, etc., is carefully dissected.

Limited though Pareto's framework for examining the contents of social life is, it is clearly an attempt to break away from the intuitive and transcendental methods of dealing with non-rational factors in behaviour. The effort to develop empirical tools for treating, among other items, the social determinants of philosophies, has moved on at a swift pace. There is, for example, no longer a need to assume with such pioneers of the *Wissenssoziologie* as Scheler (1926) and von Schelting (1929), a metaphysical pose of knowledge as a free-floating entity. The attempt to "escape from relativism" by carving the universe into material objects and moral objects, existential facts and value essences, culture and civilization, was an effort to overcome Hegel's historicism with a return to Kant's transcendental categories. This metaphysical pose was required by Scheler and von Schelting since, although they were willing to accept the relativist notion that knowledge is perspectively bound to social position and social interests, they were unwilling to accept the consequences of relativism. It is for this reason that they were compelled to bifurcate knowledge into profane and sacred aspects.

However instrumental to the growth of a sociology of knowledge were the discussions between historicists and transcendentalists, both parties to the debate assumed rather than proved the idea that the possession of social interests is a necessary impediment to the acquisition of knowledge. Such writers as Aron (1935), Popper (1952) and Frankel (1955), have shown the logical inconsistencies in assuming that the treatment of things from different or conflicting viewpoints automatically invalidates an empirical theory of truth and verification. Yet it was precisely this assumption that was common to Mannheim's "relationism" and Scheler's "relative consolidation" within a "logical hierarchy of types." (Cf. Scheler, 1924:114-17, 133.) Mannheim and Scheler offer false alternatives to the problem of knowledge because they start from the notion that empirical knowledge yields opinions rather than truths, that we are limited to relations in society and perspectives in values. Yet I do not think it fair to close this preliminary account without noting that Mannheim and Scheler were rising to the difficult task of overcoming the shortcomings in historicism by means of sociological theory, i.e., by showing the social roots of all mental life.

The difficulty in the work of Aron and Popper is that they identify the course of the sociology of knowledge with the careers of its founders, Mannheim and Scheler. In an intellectual milieu less charged with inherited metaphysical issues, the legitimate objections to relativism can be made without the wholesale dismissal of the sociology of knowledge. The sociology of knowledge offers a special order of material, having a special usefulness. And the elimination of a certain range of metaphysical problems from its domain does not effect the possibility of the sociology of knowledge making a different type of contribution to our understanding of ideas and ideologies than the founders of the discipline had in mind. In this, the sociology of knowledge stands in the same relation to literature, art, and metaphysics, as do the other social sciences. Its criteria of evidence has to be grounded in verifiable information rather than upon brilliant intuition.

Chapter IV

Philosophic Methods and
Social Understanding

The study of the content and confines of the sociology of knowledge *vis a vis* philosophy requires a differentiation between empirical science and the critical, logical appraisal of science. From the philosophic side, Lee (1949) and McKeon (1951) have explored the theoretical basis of philosophic methods. I should like to offer, from a sociological perspective, an extension of their efforts. In an investigation of the dominant methodological forms of abstract theories, a clearer view of the social genesis of ideas may be garnered. For our purpose, differences between dialectic, pragmatic, and positivist methodologies —each of which has a social prominence which may or may not be disproportionate to its philosophic worth—offers an adequate starting point.

The dialectic is essentially a way of studying the universe as a totality in process. It is an orientation toward change that attempts to internalize the causal base of the steady growth and generation of natural and social phenomena. Dialectical logic is a tool for understanding and predicting objective (particularly social) history. As such, in Lefebvre's terms, "formal logic is one of the moments in reason" (1947:145), which is to say that even logical method is subject to change and growth. Dialectics asserts the ontological priority of any meaningful methodology. This method does not so much repudiate other methodological instruments as insist on the existential truth of dialectics; the integration of objective history and human practice, change and the human transformation of change into progress.

Pragmatism, or as it has come to be refined in its evolution from

James to Bridgman—operationalism, is more a method than a new philosophic synthesis. It asserts that the dynamic object is constituted through the operations performed by man and directly experienced by man. In this sense, every technological gain is not so much a victory over nature as it is an extension of the sensory apparatus of man. In place of the dialectical relation of internal-external, pragmatic method asserts the primacy of the subject-object relation. The logic of pragmatism, if we take Dewey (1938) as representative, is no less an effort to suppress formalism than dialectics. However, instead of viewing method ontologically, as the status of the relation between perceived and perceiver, the experienced object and one who experiences, method becomes an instrument for altering and ordering things in terms of assessed human wants rather than supposed laws of nature and society. Pragmatic method further implies experience as the fundamental category of action. It relates man and nature in the great adventure of siezing the universe through the activities of human creativity. The polarizations of dialectics are drowned in the unity of human experience.

Positivist methodologies are carved into many parts, variously called conventionalism by Poincaré, phenomenalism by Ayer, logical atomism by Russell, and infinite combinations of the words empirical, logical and positivist. (Cf. Grünbaum, 1960; Cohen, 1960). While this discourages generalizations about positivism, certain broad features are held in common. Its advocates tend to agree (with Russell and Wittgenstein as notable exceptions) that method should be free from ontology of any sort. Weyl (1949) and von Mises (1951) consider dialectic as being totally outside the realm of logical relevance since it is simply a set of tautological statements. Carnap (1937) similarly considers pragmatism as a special sub-class of scientific language. Positivist method involves a complete shift from qualitative analysis, from examinations of critical changes in the structure of nature and society, to a quantitative or atomic model for representing the multiplicity of experience.

It requires no intuitive insight to realize that each of these methods is firmly involved in the level of scientific achievement of the age. Dialectics was at least broadly indebted to the discovery of differential and integral calculus, qualitative and quantitative chemistry, the development of an electromagnetic theory by Dalton, Faraday and Maxwell, and not the least, to the development of physical anthropology. (Cf. Engels, 1872-82.) Pragmatism, less concerned with the leaps and jumps in nature, paid more attention to theories of change as a whole. In Darwin's doctrine of biological evolution pragmatism found a way to preserve the value of order in a world of change. By taking the suddenness of transformation out of method, pragmatism was able to announce the possibility of social change without revolution. (Cf. Weiner, 1949.)

Positivism, basing itself on the destruction of Newtonian mechanics by Mach and Einstein, and the work of Riemann and Lobatchevski in developing non-Euclidean geometries, further explored the possibilities in formalizing method along strict empircist lines. Positivists reasoned that a consistent methodology should be uncommitted to theories of nature or society. A logical method could make no commitment to a logic with ontology or to a mathematics dependent on sensations. Method, in short, had to be *wertfrei*, isolated from broad theories of nature, society and ethics. (Cf. Nagel, 1957:55ff.) Positivism has remained ambiguous as to the existential status of processes, but it rallied about the notion that a meaningful rendering of such processes had to empty itself of apriori judgments concerning reality. Operational definitions are not without value, but they simply involve a subjectivization of experience, instead of a mathematical and logical rendering of events.

These comments on alternative philosophic methods are compressed sketches, and are not to be taken as a measure of their actual worth. However, two things can be said of the three methods discussed: (a) they point in different and not necessarily compatible directions; (b) they all differ from scientific method in that each asserts an epistemological superiority quite outside the domain of either experiment or evidence. This is not to say that the scientific method is either logically or morally superior to the dialectical, pragmatic or positivist methodologies, or that they display no points in common, merely that it is different and that, to the degree the sociology of knowledge employs scientific method, it must diverge from a commitment to any of the inherited philosophic methods.

A primary element in the methodology of the sociology of knowledge is the social typing of philosophic methods. This itself may take a "philosophic" form as in the earlier writings of Landsberg (1931) and Dilthey (1922), or it may take a "quantitative" form as in the more recent studies of Abel (1948) and Adler (1954). Whatever the form, what is involved is examining the social foundation of differing philosophic methods. What results are forthcoming is, of course, relative to the object under investigation and the perspicacity of the investigator. What the sociological typing of philosophies assumes is only that there are socially definable variables, not the primacy of any given philosophic method or theory.

Here we are on dangerous ground, since each of the aforementioned methodologies has or had an important role in shaping the sociology of knowledge. Yet the history of science has repeatedly demonstrated the possibility, if not the inevitability, of a scientific discipline attaining maturity in revolt against its philosophic birth. The first real stage, therefore, in the separation of the sociology of knowledge from philosophy is to demonstrate that the latter is indeed open to social study, and open in such a way as to show the value basis and partisanship of philosophic methods. A brief sociological excursion into dialectics, pragmatism and positivism should illustrate the soundness of such a position.

The dialectical method is presently a social force for a variety of moral and political reasons. The internalization of causal relations compels men to search within the framework of existing social arrangements for the sources of their difficulties. The dialectical method did more than react to the existence of economic exploitation and psychological alienation. In showing how they relate to each other, dialectical philosophy offered a solution to exploitation and alienation based on their driving force to seek "its other"—a non-exploitative, organic civilization. (Cf. Lukacs, 1923; Moore, 1957; ch. 4.) The doctrine of man fashioning his own future out of the materials given in the present replaced the older mechanical, chiliastic vision of man escaping his torment by a complete overturning of the present. (Cf. Childe, 1936: ch. 1.) Progress came to be defined as the unity of evolution and revolution, tradition and change, not simply as the utopian suppression of one side of the historical coin at the expense of the other. The materialist dialectic of Marx saw itself as scientific precisely in its capacity to see history, not as the alternation of good and evil, but as the record of human achievement, however partial such achievement might be. To be sure, the very incompleteness of real history was considered a factor driving men eternally onward and upward.

As Plekhanov saw (1895: ch. 5), the dialectical method could preserve the notion of the lawful character of social evolution, without destroying individual initiative. The dialectic method is a determinism which attempts to transcend mechanism in social affairs by including men in every calculation. The idea of man as a transforming agent became the practical expression of overcoming indolence and quietude when overwhelmed by continuous independent operation of social law. In its Marxian form, the direction of human strivings is held to be subordinate to iron laws of history, knowable by a scientific elite constituted as a political party having as the source of knowledge the experience of an oppressed economic class.

The relation of cooperation to coercion, which replaced the abstract metaphysical theory of the relation of free will to necessity, was the basis of most revolutionary social doctrines during the past one hundred years. The ends of political action were viewed as predictable in the same way that experiments with electricity are predictable. Whether the transformation of energy is studied, or the transformation of economics is studied, increased knowledge means getting where we want to go more rapidly. The dialectic method grants that the progressive development of society can be impeded and even temporarily frustrated, but barring catastrophic events, the human enterprise is realized through the dialectical process of change. In such a methodology, the task is, to accelerate the process by which the march into the future can be carried further.

Dialectics was a clear breach in what, up to the time of Kant, Hegel and Marx, appeared to be the invincibility of mechanism in social thought. Dialectics represented an all-out effort to reconcile the man of reason with the man of action. Its power to give romantic expression to mechanical occurrences at the macroscopic and microscopic levels of nature (i.e., atomic events as the external appearance of intensive action within each particle), gave followers of the dialectic the feeling that physical science sanctioned the types of polarized, oppositional struggle dialectics advocated for the political and economic realms. Every quantitative event, every statistical isolate, and every electromagnetic charge, represented a qualitative and dynamic force. Only passivity, only a solipsistic form of empiricism could fail to yield a like view of social organization. The very tools of science on the dialectical view represented a stage in the historical development of human nature and human consciousness. The tautological, self-fulfilling prophecies involved in the dialectic, were washed away in the drama of helping to make predictions come true.

Dialectical philosophies tended to think of truth as itself something partial, something being made in the process of history. Change alone was absolute. The dialectical method was that instrument which constantly presses beyond the *status quo* into the polarized units of society generating further change. That the dialectic offered no criteria of internal controls or confirmation was not considered a damaging argument to its value. This became its virtue, since every event could be interpreted as a proof of the dialectic at work. The dialectic gave insight. The society of dialecticians could claim, what the society of psychoanalysts were later to claim, a special ability to interpret, predict and control not open to all men. Since each social prediction involved political action, questions as to the reliability or authenticity of the dialectical method tended to be lost in the miasma of practical political programmes.

At all levels of society, the dialectic operated to revolutionize human attitudes to change. It was a method which could be employed and understood by an *avant-garde* concerned with social betterment and it could even stimulate physicists to rethink basic premises as to the structure of the natural world. Dialectics was an insistence upon the universality of change in a world which up to the 19th century was restricted by mechanical invariants on one hand, and religious apocalypses on the other. Sociologically, the dialectic method became a basis for renewed study of political elites, mass revolutions, propaganda techniques, and the behaviour of crowds. That its method allowed for but a single possible ultimate political conclusion only strengthened its adherents in the view that social action and scientific prediction are compatible.

The pragmatic method, no less than dialectical approaches, centered around the issue of change and in finding truth in concrete individual behaviour. But in its rejection of the objective and historical aspects of change, pragmatism issued into theories of reform rather than into revolutionary ideologies. The displacement of the objective dialectic, working its way mysteriously through society, issued into the idea that revolution is, at best, but one possible adjustment to a hostile environment, rather than the central agency of social change.

The notion of man as being part of the natural fabric of life flowed from a philosophy based on evolutionary biology, from a conception of social conflict that held change to be natural and gradual. Adaptation in dealings with nature and adjustment in dealings with men keynoted the pragmatic methodology. Education was to render this adjustment—adaptation formula even more calm. Here too, as in the dialectic, a wide latitude of action was to be granted, since pragmatism made central the plural possibilities of social change. It offered a picture of nature as essentially indeterminate and pliable, subject to the direct wishes of men rather than the questionable attribute of either universal or historical laws. (Cf. James, 1907:41ff.)

Truth itself became plastic, identifiable with the willed strivings of men rather than with imagined iron laws of society. The liberal revolt, which commenced with James' critique of scholasticism and Cartesianism, ended in a prosaic search for the middle ground ideology with Dewey. The middle ground methodology of pragmatism asked not whether nature or society permitted a constant search for options, but whether it would be in the interests of men to seek evolutionary or revolutionary paths to social salvation. The method of intelligence clearly dictated the painless way of changing social relations. But this method assumed a plurality of possibilities that it never demonstrated existed. Pragmatic method did not deny the theory of progress. Its method is an extension to the social realm of a biological theory of progress. What it did reject was the idea that determinism was compatible with social advancement.

The symbol of the instrument corresponded to the widened employment of technology in the industrial life of America. Instrumentalism presaged an era when man not only makes himself, but does so spontaneously and in terms of a freely willed selection of experienced social materials. The pragmatic method, which remained the kernel of instrumental philosophies, showed the possibility of connecting the world of diverse experiences without necessarily determining what the contents or worth of that experience might become. Liberalism supplied social answers to the widespread demand for radical change by selecting for itself a manipulative method which saw in education and its institutions the prime form of realizing social and political change gradually.

Positivist methodology represented more than a philosophic revolt against the traditional ontological opposition between materialism and idealism, empiricism and rationalism. At the sociological level it was the sustained effort to separate social description from social prescription. The isolation of meaning from morals, the reduction of the latter to a series of emotive projections, provided a method supposedly free of value predicates. That the performance never quite lives up to the pose is a consequence of the necessity of the positivists to bring certain values into focus through the back door. Truth itself, without wish fulfillments and anthro-projections, was itself considered liberating. In his survey of the analytic movement, Nagel (1936) speaks of the "sociological motivations at Vienna." He goes on to note that the *formal* ethical neutrality of positivism was in practice "a potent intellectual explosive"—given a social climate of economic floundering and political reaction in Central Europe. The attack on obscurantism was thus filled with a rich ethical content. The *Wiener Kreis*, in its zeal to eliminate pomp and ceremony from philosophy and obscurantism from political doctrines, offered the most damaging self-criticism of the notion of a *wertfrei* method.

The initial fact to note is the anti-mystical orientation of positivist method; its insistence upon an empirically verifiable theory of truth and a logical theory of language. The strict formalism of positivist methodology, the mathematical and physical training of its adherents, tended to disguise its social origins in the professional middle classes who sought a place in the scientific world. Philosophy as higher technology was erected as a buffer against the charge that philosophy is either common-sense or uncommon nonsense. This widespread popular opinion, shared by many in the learned professions, lowered the status of philosophy considerably. The logical, linguistic apparatus of positivist methodology shielded it from such charges. Positivism achieved a unique professional gloss by mimetically reproducing the claims of natural science. Positivists constituted themselves into small communities: the Vienna Circle, the Cambridge group, the Berlin Circle, the Warsaw logicians. Their alienated social condition during the emergence of European fascism fostered in them distinctive group attitudes: members, tests of admittance, roles of members, and norms of social relations.

What did positivist methodology offer? What were the social determinants in its position? In the first place, positivism offered an intellectualist solution to social problems. It permits us to talk only of the meaningful, not of the desirable. Positivist currents were uniform in their search for universal validity formally, in a way not dependent upon an empirical or moral content. It was to be an extension of mathematics to the study of the logical components of ordinary language. The proof that a problem is genuine was held to be the ability to structure it symbolically, i.e., logically. Such a methodology reveals an obvious mistrust for things not open to ordinary forms of logical symbolization, such as poetry and literature, although, parenthetically we might add that scholars like Richards (1929) have tried mightily to extend the canons of positivist methodology to the arts. A subjective theory of knowledge emerged out of a method which believed only in the reality of sense perceptions and pure logical forms. The mathematical ordering of experience involved a theory of truth as the coherence of propositions, rather than as the correspondence of experience and reality. Formal verification became thought of as the real (if not the only) task of the sciences.

The methodological credo of positivism, that propositions about science contain nothing but protocols about immediate experience, is in its own way as tautological as the statements made by dialectic and pragmatic methods. For as Reichenbach (1936) pointed out, scientific propositions make assertions about the past and the future, no less than the present. Thus the practice of science insists on a good deal more than propositions having a symmetrical form placed between quotation marks. The zeal with which positivism pursued its goal of purging philosophy from anything other than a system of definitions is indicative of the extra-scientific values at stake (cf. Ramsey, 1931); values which are essentially geared to solve social problems of the intellectual in a technicians' world.

Correspondence between function and fact, between things symbolized and the process of symbolization, was consigned to metaphysical purgatory. Intellect became separated from methodology, since no dependence or correlation of mind and nature was considered necessary. Indeed, the early pioneers of positivism, Wittgenstein, Schlick, and Russell, have been repeatedly criticized for not offering a complete enough distinction between logical coherence and epistemic correspondence. The formalization of method into a metalanguage constituted a rupture with both the dialectic method and the pragmatic method of experience. Methodology became another word for computation. Answers are guaranteed since the information declared meaningful results from answering only those questions which are open to empirical solution.

Positivist method realized at least one central aim: that method should be so constructed as to allow for internal validation. The price, willingly paid, for realizing this aim was abandoning social prescription. Political science became isolated from politics as such; sociology became segregated from social welfare; and economic theory became isolated from the economic system. Of course, positivism merely reflected the actual disintegration of the nineteenth century ideal of the man of knowledge as also the man of social practice. Positivism enshrined a situation rather than created a new methodology.

Value neutrality went up as a cry in the night, itself to become an ultimate value. The purer methodology became in positivist thought, the less applications it seemed to have to those questions of value the philosopher was dedicated to resolve. This factor, coupled as it was with the inability to recognize its own valuational base, made positivism a tool lacking in human purpose. The intellectual became transformed into an ally of the machine. The positivist was to be the mechanic making sure that the parts of the machine were in logical order.

These sociological comments and criticisms of philosophic methods do not detract from their contribution to the growth of a scientific sociology of knowledge. Dialectics fostered the study of the historical and economic content of ideas; pragmatics focused on the importance of irrationalism in the formation of idea systems and political slogans; and positivist methodology contributed to the sociology of knowledge by noting that factual statements and moral statements have distinct psychological sources and implications.

The main point, however, is that a sociology of knowledge necessarily employs a method common to all science, and is thus distinct from philosophical methods. While it has historical roots in philosophy, it is at the same time a primary instrument for the social evaluation of these inherited methods. That the success of the sociology of knowledge in explaining the ideological, religious and scientific components of philosophic methods has thus far been tentative, is more a reflection of the youth of the discipline than a critique of its worth.

The sociology of knowledge helps clarify the causes and consequences of philosophic methods, and in so doing explains how the method of science is distinct from and logically superior to the philosophical perspectives developed in the quest for knowledge. (Cf. Kaufman, 1944; and Lundberg, 1947.) Beyond this, the sociology of knowledge can determine both the past and present conditions of the rise of scientific method in the very process of employing its rules. Admittedly, the practical goals of sociology are quite apart from the moral goals of practice—but in so far as the former may inform and guide the latter, sociology cannot be said to be without value predicates.

Chapter V

Operational Philosophy and Functional Sociology

Iɴ examining philosophic methods we drew the distinction between the tautological nature of all philosophic methods and the empirical nature of scientific method, with its criteria of verification, explanation and prediction. The worth of philosophic systems stems from their ability to employ method to establish internal coherence. The logical correlation of ideas with other ideas is its central aim. The scientific system, on the other hand, remains constantly open, in that its materials are drawn from a universe in flux. Such a distinction between science and philosophy is itself primitive. Even if we take Popper's (1952: ch. 23) notion that the proof of the superiority of scientific method is in its consequences for controlling events, the problem remains as to why the pragmatic ideal of consequences should be rated as logically superior.

This would indicate that questions of value can be excluded from sociology only at the price of finding it reduced to vulgar empiricism which satisfies only formal criteria of evidence, doing little more than tallying data with clarifying assumptions. What remains is sociologically trivial, since the basis for projecting and predicting remains a blind article. On the other hand, to place value questions in the forefront, and treat them by intuition, leaves us without a sociological science. To make every factual question into an ethical question is to frustrate the practical character of a science and return us to a metaphysical impasse. The tragedy, as Mills (1959) has taken note of, is that contemporary sociology is seemingly hung on a choice of false alternatives: either narrow empiricism or grand designs. The job of a useful

53

philosophy is not to take sides in such matters, but to explore the implications of all alternatives available to the social sciences—true and false.

The preconditions of sociology have remained largely unexamined by the sociologist. Like primitive numbers in mathematics, the entire axiological framework is taken to rest upon its operational worth. But what is the operational worth of a sociology which mimetically reproduces the idea of physical models? Is it not the task of philosophy to see what intelligible meaning can be assigned to the most sacred canons in social science? It has become painfully clear that the very attempt to make the language of social research free of values by erecting mathematical and physical models, is itself a conditioned response to a world which pays a premium price for technological manipulation.

This push to confine the study of mass behaviour to the measurements of parameters involved in differential equations has led sociology perilously close to the reduction of the word "mass" to mean a small group in which certain relations between all pairs of individuals in such a group can be studied. (Cf. Rapoport, 1959: ch. 11.) Here I think the role of the philosopher becomes apparent. The simple pragmatic success of the sociology of small groups needs to be questioned. For if the small group notion involves the implicit claim that the phenomena of sociological investigations are of atomic or subatomic proportions, the philosopher needs to know the extent to which such entities are valid. The mere exploration of the unconscious ground of present-day sociology offers a rich vein of philosophical and logical investigation. (Cf. Brodbeck, 1959: Ch. 12.)

A parallel function for philosophy is the study of the relation between perceptions experientially received and conceptions logically formed. Philosophy can supply adequate criteria of meaning in the selection of socially viable categories. This involves a sifting of the empirical and rational elements entering into each social science statement. Merton's functional sociology may have great practical use in the study of different cultures, yet it is perfectly clear as Nagel (1957:247-83) and Hempel (1959:271-307) indicate, that the concept of function in sociology has been built up from physiological and biological models, in which the notions of teleology, i.e., metaphysical purpose, are central. (Cf. Chapter IX.) Functionalism as a sociological credo is, therefore, not a direct consequence of observations, but rather an indirect consequence of philosophical inference and judgment.

The purpose of this sort of philosophical study of sociology is not to tyrannize but to clarify the principles of social science. It is absurd to speak of philosophy as a superior enterprise to sociology, since the former is a logical, rational discipline, where sociology is essentially descriptive and empirical. Such a position entails the negation of philosophy in its Platonic form as something soaring above and embracing the empirical and mathematical sciences. But contrary to Whitehead, philosophy is not a synonym for Plato. The uses of philosophy as a logical clearing house are manifest to any approach that does not descend to pure sensationalism. However, when philosophy attempts to stand above the sciences, to dictate the conditions of empirical research, it becomes formal metaphysics; shaping the contours of life to fit the needs of legends. The notion of philosophy as Queen Bee may fit well with authoritarian modes of political ideology, but it has been noted that the price of such an imperial notion of philosophy is the frustration and flagellation of the social sciences. (Cf. Wetter, 1952: Pt. II, Ch. 5; Horowitz, 1957b.)

Metaphysics is no longer a direct grappling with nature as it was in antiquity. It has surrendered any claims of description in favor of psychological accounts of nothingness, as in Heidegger's system (1929). Science is mocked for wishing to know nothing of Nothing, in a last ditch effort to save the gods at the expense of men. It is not positivism which has isolated metaphysics from reality by distinguishing between description and prescription. It is simply revealing the state to which metaphysical thinking has fallen during this century.

Consider the traditional "four fields" of philosophy: logic, ethics, epistemology and esthetics. It is a commonplace that to the degree these special preserves of past philosophic hunting grounds establish an empirical content and suitable methodological criteria, they move away from philosophy as such. What is left to traditional systems of philosophy is, in effect, only the history of these fields prior to their becoming rigorous enough to abide by the canons of scientific method. In this situation, philosophy has survived by separating itself from metaphysics, by showing the ultimate questions to be the meaningless questions.

The relinquishing by philosophy of pretentious claims to empirical priority gives it an ability to treat problems of meaning and truth which in the past it was unable to examine because of its missionary attitude to knowledge of more humble sorts. In the new situation, philosophy is able to provide the social sciences with the same guidance that mathematics offers the physical sciences, a reservoir of logical relations that can be used in framing hypotheses having explanatory and predictive value. Beyond this, philosophy may urge the social sciences forward by asking the type of question that falls outside the present scope of social inquiry, but within its potential domain of relevance. In this connection, it might be noted that the theory of games was a mathematical discovery long before its uses in political science were exploited. Likewise, Kant formulated the nebular hypothesis, according to which the solar system was evolved from a rotating mass of incandescent gas, nearly a half century before its scientific value was made plain by Laplace in his *Système du Monde*. This does not mean that philosophy resolves the problems it generates, any more so than Riemann's geometry settled the physical status of the space-time continuum. But the forceful presentation of new issues for the sciences to work on is itself a monumental task.

To those raised on Marcel's *Homo Viator* and Heidegger's *das Nichtige*, this may seem a modest role for philosophy. However, modesty and triviality are different qualities. Philosophy conceived of as servant to the sciences might appear as less dramatic than philosophy which jeers as the sciences evolve. The ceaseless effort to understand and measure the distance mankind has traversed since its primitive anthropological status offers a more durable sort of drama. By clarifying fundamental premises in the social sciences, and defining the logical problems emergent at the borderlands of each new scientific discipline, philosophy can offer the sort of distinction that can accelerate growth in human understanding. Philosophy can prevent the working scientist from becoming slothful and self-content by noting the assumptions and level at which a hypothesis or theory is framed. The dissection of scientific theory, the examination of a theory from the vantage-points of language, epistemology, and ethics, is itself a distinct contribution to knowledge, no less so because of its removal from empirical research.

The realm of science, whatever the degree of precision in formulations, covers the range of prediction and explanation. (Cf. Hempel and Oppenheim, 1948:135-75.) Whatever philosophy is conceived to be, its rationalist, logistic attitude to evidence should make it clear that it is something other than science. For some forms of philosophy, this very division between the empirical and the rational becomes a sign of the metaphysical superiority of the latter. Bergson and Leroy announce that "the secret is the center of a philosophy" and thereafter a hundred followers declare secrecy a higher verity. This is simply a confession of intellectual sterility spruced up to look virtuous. For as Merleau-Ponty indicated (1953), it is not the secret which is important, but the removal of secrecy. In this, philosophy and science share a common goal. The hypostatization of the secret nonetheless guarantees that the division of analytical and synthetic philosophies shall not be overcome by even the most persuasive argument; for this division is but an abstract representation of the social struggle between mysticism and science.

The mystification of metaphysical systems does not imply the demise of philosophy, only the close of a philosophic age which demanded metaphysics to be rational and logical. The tenacity with which present metaphysical attitudes fetishize private intuition offers the strongest evidence that the gulf between scientific and delphic ways of philosophizing is built into the present conflict over the limits and purpose of science, religion and ideology. (Cf. McGlynn: 1958.) Scientific systems, and this includes even the relation of mechanist to relativist physics, are built upon, refined and corrected. Philosophic systems, by the very nature of their completeness, are overthrown by rival systems. In addition to the incompleteness of science and the completeness of metaphysics, they differ in that science is essentially descriptive, while philosophy in its inherited forms, tends to be goal-oriented, teleological and prescriptive. The threadbare notion that belief, unlike behaviour, is not subject to objective analysis, has placed intuitive metaphysics squarely against the sociology of knowledge, since it is precisely the job of the sociology of knowledge to treat beliefs as social facts no less viable than social behaviour.

When dealing with the actual relation of philosophy to the sociology of knowledge, or better the role of philosophy in assisting research on the social sources of ideas, one has to become necessarily selective. Certain features we have touched upon: philosophy as a logical, deductive system from which a social science methodology can be built up; philosophic analysis of the assumptions and presumptions of the social sciences; and philosophy as a guide to possible integration of supposedly disparate sociological investigations.

The objection will be raised that the most important role of philosophy in relation to social science has been omitted, namely the status of ultimate value questions and norms operative in the social sciences. Specifically, it will be asked whether the "real" questions people ask are not the "ultimate" questions that social science finds itself impotent in the face of. What then is the status of such questions as: is society the ground of human existence or a means to an individual goal? Do societies develop according to cosmic patterns or are they subject only to the free choice of individuals? Does society really exist as an entity over and above the agglomeration of men? I think it must be said that, contrary to metaphysical insistence, these are questions so framed as to defy either empirical exploration or rational solutions. As Simmel (1908) and Dilthey (1922) indicated, questions of whether the value of life is individual or social are not questions, but assertions of faith made to appear as legitimate questions. Such pseudo-questions assume that answers of concrete significance can be supplied to statements involving undefined universals. Social theory has no more right to expect results from meaningless questions, than physics has the right to expect a theological solution to the wave-particle controversy.

It is not that such questions are not asked. It is rather that introducing them into social analysis reflects not so much a search for truth as for certainty. An operational approach to sociology can never expect abstract certainty, since it is certainty which every new discovery in science either replaces or reshapes. To raise the added objection that men require certainty on psychological grounds, answers to ultimate questions having an irrational rather than scientific basis, is in a real sense to undermine the objection itself. For what concerns all scientific disciplines is precisely that which can be captured for the rational, i.e., for the scientific determination of what in past ages was considered ultimate and irrational.

A philosophy which attempts to supply ultimate answers in an ultimate way reveals its acquiescence in the shortcomings of men, an impatience with partial, tentative solutions. Men have always lived in a tentative world, and in suspension of ultimate judgments where and when necessary. Uncertainty overcoming itself is the precondition of the quest for new and more precise information about the world. Without such uncertainty we are left with a set of dogmas and myths. The functional interplay of philosophy and science should, as a minimum, guarantee a meaningful option to myth-making.

A degree of indefiniteness is a salutary condition for the growth of science. Absolute certainty is simply a condition of intellectual atrophy. The changing contents of reality require a view of experience consonant with the facts. The role of philosophy in this is to present the actual problems and logical paradoxes of the sciences for clear and immediate attention. For philosophy to do more, to attempt total resolutions of social problems as if they were special cases of a metaphysical system, is to invite a justified ridicule from scientific quarters. For philosophy to do less, to abandon the field of values and norms to the less informed, is a sign of indolence and dotage which is no less subject to ridicule and repudiation. (Cf. Davis, 1957.)

The European sociological tradition, nourished as it was on inherited metaphysical credos, has tended to pay uncritical tribute to speculative and intuitive systems. This is sometimes done from a justifiable concern for the blind elements in empirical sociologies, and at other times from an unjustifiable deference to the romanticist view of science as inhuman and devoid of general values.

Max Scheler, for example, attempts to extend a noumenalist

theory of personality into a general theory of society. *Herrschaft und Unterwerfung*, domination and subjugation become reified into eternal human types. Scheler's novel expression of the power thesis has its opposite in man's search for a spiritual alternative to power. Philosophy becomes man's eternal search for freedom, and sociology becomes the expression of this search in the affairs of family, community and state. (Cf. Scheler, 1928.) But this amalgam of philosophy and sociology only results in enshrining theology as the highest form of knowledge; a large price to pay for doing away with the exaggerations of narrow empiricism.

Georges Gurvitch, no less concerned with slaying the dragons of sociological empiricism (1955: ch. 9), offers a secular option to a scientific philosophy. Offering no distinctions between social philosophy and sociology, Gurvitch has no difficulty in maintaining the need to unite factual evidence and philosophic ideals. This done, the problem of prescription vanishes for sociology, the way the problem of description vanishes for the philosopher. This is a genial view, resting on the broadmindedness of the sociologist and the desire for the concrete which is assumed to motivate the philosopher. The difficulty with this is that paying *hommage* to philosophy is a different order of problem than finding a genuine place for it in an age of social science. To assert the usefulness of philosophy for sociology is not a substitute for demonstrating such use. Yet this is all that the humanism of Gurvitch allows (1957).

The philosopher might be wiser to heed Wittgenstein's epigram before deciding the best relationship between sociology and philosophy. "The philosopher's treatment of a question is like the treatment of an illness" (1953). If I interpret this rightly, this means that philosophy is called into play when crises in social theory reveal themselves in the practice of explanation, prediction and control. In these situations philosophy may act as a cleansing agent for the logic and language of sociology. This is what is implied by considering philosophy as the logic of social science. Insistence upon a more inclusive picture, to maintain that philosophy mysteriously harmonizes (Scheler) or humanizes (Gurvitch) sociology, is another form of expressing discontent with the methodology and findings of social science.

From the perspective of a scientific world, Dewey is correct in insisting that the survival of philosophy depends upon the distance it puts between itself and its metaphysical, dualistic inheritance (1944). Likewise, from the same perspective, the real future of sociology depends on its willingness to submit its method and assumptions to philosophical analysis. As Adler (1957) indicates, it is time for sociology to discard the ballast of inflated language and esoteric speculation its founders were encumbered with, and strive for a humanism that will not choke off scientific studies of the societies men live in and strive for.

Chapter VI

Science, Criticism and the Sociology of Knowledge

CRITICISM of the sociology of knowledge has been legion. Of these there have been three lines of attack that deserve serious philosophical attention.

First Criticism: Social science is inexact, whereas natural science is exact. This approach, which tends to become an indictment of sociology as a whole and not just the sociology of knowledge, is fallacious on two counts. First, the question of precision in science is one of methodology. There are indeed differences in in the precision of physics and sociology, but this is due to the present level of procedural and predictive capacities of physics *vis a vis* sociology, and not to any intrinsic differences between the methodologies of the various sciences. Those making the charges against sociology as a science usually have as an underlying motive the replacement of science with intuition as the basic way to social understanding. Helmer and Rescher (1959) have made clear that social science cannot be separated from physical science on methodological grounds. The second difficulty in such a line of reasoning is that precision in analysis is related to the number of "free" variables in any given problem situation; and since human society involves a great deal more of these complex factors than either inanimate nature or even animal societies, it is clear that prediction at these lower levels of existence will usually be more exact. Although where there exists a comparable control of the variables, as in certain small-scale economic predictions and in mechanical engineering predictions, both of which include measurements of probability and deviations, degrees of exactness are also comparable. We are thus obliged to consider the question of precision relative to the technical and historical stage each science has arrived at, and not impose upon nature the labored distinction between physical and social.

Second Criticism: One can measure behaviour, but not beliefs. This criticism, made most often by those working in the older social and behavioral sciences, tends to erect a dualism between behaviour and belief for which there is no evidence. Of course, not every belief is translated into an act, and not every act is capable of accounting in terms of belief. This does not, however, vitiate the fact that beliefs (rational and irrational) can be treated as facts for the scientist. And while it can be argued that the *observation* of facts does not entail the *measurement* of facts, the purposes of science—prediction and explanation—would be thoroughly frustrated if facts were viewed simply as raw data not subject to inclusion in theories and laws. To be sure, the measure of how mature a social study of knowledge is would have to be in terms of how precise explanation and prediction is in relating behaviour patterns to ideological configurations. What seems to underscore this criticism of the sociology of knowledge is that the very introduction of ideas into the social matrix creates chaos and caprice. But this line of criticism confuses complexity with chaos.

Third Criticism: Social science can only distinguish between opinions, and hence establish the relativity of opinions. It can establish no truths and no laws. Much comment of *Wissenssoziologie* has centered on the impossibility of taking a non-ideological position on ideological issues. This highly respected comment is transparently thin in that its guarded assumption amounts to the assertion that social science is without a legal status. The refutation of this position does not entail acceptance of the *wertfrei intelligenz* put forth by Alfred Weber (1934) and Mannheim (1935, 1953). What is being noted is the common sense fact that the social scientist *qua* scientist, is concerned with both explanation and prediction. At present, the sociology of knowledge is better able to explain the sources of ideologies than to predict the idea configurations which will come about through changes in the social structure. But here again, what we have is a degree of scientific maturity, not an intrinsic philosophic obstacle to the formation of a sociology of knowledge.

There is a distinction between objective truth (the inter-subjective verification of data) and privately held opinions. But simply because the sociology of knowledge operates within the former is no reason to reject the possibility of locating the basis of opinions, values and ethical judgments. (Cf. Edel, 1955.) We can certify objectively (or inter-subjectively as observers) that there is a certain subjectively structured fact. To say this implies that the sociology of knowledge has as a fundamental orientation the discovery of both the social roots of error and of truth, fact and opinion. However, such a perspective does not commit us to the view of Stark (1958: ch. 4), which conceives of this dual role in historical terms only; denying the conceptual significance of truth and error. What I have in mind requires no metaphysical superstructure. Simply, within the sociology of knowledge, the object under study largely determines the mechanisms of exploration. Those concerned with the history of science will more often be drawn to investigate the social conditions which allow for the "production of truths," whereas those interested in political and economic history will generally be concerned with the sources of ideological distortions sanctified by this political regime or that economic system.

The critical function of the sociology of knowledge enables it to act as a catalyst in the integration of social science disciplines into a common, interlocked network. The most significant way to settle the question of the theoretical possibility of the sociology of knowledge is to demonstrate the practical impossibility of social science without it. While the work of Child (1941, 1947), Hinshaw (1943), and Lavine (1944) have shown the disparity between criticism of Mannheim and Scheler, and the sociology of knowledge as such, it remains a central fact that the most striking evidence for the sociology of knowledge has thus far been supplied by political scientists, psychologists and economists.

Veblen (1899) and Weber (1904) illustrated the potency of bringing to the foreground the interconnection between economy and ideology. The nature of a productive system may properly be a question determined by a pure theory of economics. However, there are a host of consequent issues not so easily determined on a non-attitudinal basis. The problem of consumer satisfaction and demand, for example, is essentially sociological. Thus Weber and Veblen could inquire into the larger consequences of an industrial exchange economy: the social basis of contractual agreements, non-income factors in the distribution of industrial privileges, the role of industry in political elites, the constantly changing notion of "essential" and "non-essential" goods, attitudinal shifts between employers and employees, the status role of professional and labor organizations, and the relation of leisure to conspicuous and vicarious consumption. These are but some of the ways in which a sociology of knowledge was employed in the social sciences before it was crystallized into an independent discipline.

It was, after all, in the economic system of Marx (1867) that the first concerted effort to relate economy and ideology was undertaken. It was in Marx's discussion of the relation of man to machine in capitalist industry that the attendant concepts of alienation, fetishism, and mental production were first expounded. In this connection, it might be noted how backward the formulations of Plekhanov and Bukharin were in relating economics to a sociology of knowledge. (Cf. esp. Bukharin, 1935.) When they assert that sociology is simply a myth of the bourgeoisie, a device to disparage the real science of society, Marxian economics, they are merely revealing a misunderstanding not only of sociology, but of Marxism, i.e., the effort to reveal the social ramifications of human practice. (Cf. Labedz, 1958: ch. 21.)

Whatever the terminological shifts in economy from Marx to Keynes, economists have not ceased being interested in the relation of economic systems and ideologies. The recent efforts of Schumpeter (1949) and Myrdal (1944, 1958) offer convincing evidence as to the utility of the sociology of knowledge for economic theory. Their work in establishing the reciprocity of value standards and monetary policy, the distinction between programmes and prognosis, the role of attitudes and entrenchment in forming classes, and in the relationship of empirical facts to personal desires, has served to carry Weber's *Sozialpolitik* a step further. Myrdal in particular has been deeply concerned with the possibilities of developing an objective science of economics on the basis of sociological findings. Schumpeter's efforts have been more concentrated, directed as they have been in locating those ideological mechanisms that may, under certain conditions enhance or retard social democracy.

The area of political science, which bears a close operational kinship to the sociology of knowledge (despite emphasis on institutions in the former and upon ideas in the latter), offers an additionally large fund of expert information to draw upon. Even if we restrict ourselves to the modern period, ignoring the contributions made to classical political theory by Machiavelli, Hobbes, Rousseau and Hegel, it is manifest that the political anchors of the sociology of knowledge require the findings of political science. The changing juridical commitments of specific political structures examined by Schlesinger (1945) and Kelsen (1955), the study of oligarchic tendencies in political party organizations made by Michels (1912), the relationships of mass and class galvanizing political action made by Sorel (1908) and Pareto (1916), serve to illustrate some major convergence points between political theory and the sociology of knowledge.

There are also the concentrated studies which have been particularly fruitful for those concerned with questions of the social determination of knowledge. There is the attempt at an empirical typology of elites made by Mills (1955) and Lasswell (1952), symposia on mass communication, authoritarian personalities, popular culture, and national ideologies, edited by Adorno (1950), Gross (1948), and Rosenberg (1958), detailed examinations of political belief and participation offered by Berelson (1952), Gottfried (1955) and Davies (1954), and the relation of consensus to conflict in political sociology offered by Lipset (1959). Unless one has private reasons for insisting that the sociology of knowledge can never amount to more than a random dipping into "an ocean of pyschic events," it should be plain that this branch of sociology has nourished a good deal of work in political science.

The geographic movement of political science from Europe to the United States has stimulated a concentration on technical problems and away from larger theoretical concerns. While there are those, like Leo Strauss (1959: ch. 1), who continue to handle the big issues of the relation of State and society, civilization and the individual, freedom and authority, political theory has, for the most part, shifted into technical analysis of the structural components of political and social institutions. Even Strauss admits that "political philosophy does not exist any more, except as matter for burial, i.e., for historical research, or else as a theme of weak and unconvincing protestations." Unfortunately, the replacement of political philosophy by political science, has not so much solved the older problems as declared them meaningless. As a result, political science, like more recent efforts at an empiricist sociology of knowledge, tends to lapse into the trivial, into a form of quantitative analysis that is intellectually sterile. Increasingly, the manipulative aspects of analysis have replaced the search for those laws of explanation and prediction that could bring some order into the social sciences. If this has been more apparent in political science than in the sociology of knowledge, it is due to the more immediate use-value of the former, not to anything unique to its labors.

Despite the excessive manipulative orientation of political science, it has offered the sociology of knowledge correlations of political structure and human motivation that are of the first order of importance. We have been freed from the nineteenth century mechanism which insisted on a single causative agent in the production of political action. It is now realized that political behaviour has diverse motivational springs, economic, mythic, instinctual and at times directly religious. The rise of neo-Freudian psychoanalysis intensified the pluralism of political science, creating at times some high order exaggerations. Typical of the exaggerated efforts to escape mechanism in political thinking are Lasswell's characterological types: the connection between a pacifist and an acute castration complex, an anarchist leader who displays an intense father-hatred and thus anti-state views, the religious zealot who finds in politics compensation for a guilt complex. The implication of such efforts is plainly to turn every form of political radicalism into a form of neurotic compulsion. Such thinking has its parallels in all ages of intense social struggle, where the conservative party is to be found scorning the "enthusiasts" and their devilish motivations. Nonetheless, Lasswell's approach has led to a reconsideration of Nietzschean hero types in terms of more common human types. (Cf. Lasswell, 1930.)

The collapse of mechanism in the social sciences has not had the effect of throwing everything into a Jamesian "wide open universe." Social science retains as its ideal the determination of events in the most precise way the evidence allows. Paradoxically, the end of mechanism, of the insistence that the goals of future society are predictable *en toto,* has made possible a greater degree of social determinism by revealing hitherto uncharted aspects of political behaviour. The fact that these aspects involve the role of ideas and ideologies has only served to broaden the base of social science, not to a reduction in the predictive aspects of either sociology or political science.

In addition to economics and political science, psychology and psychoanalysis have come to play an increasing role in the study of ideologies. Particularly important up to now has been the discovery of the relation of psychic deviants and the emergence of ethnocentric ideologies. (Cf. Levinson, 1950.) The successful efforts made in this direction under the supervision of Muensterberger, Róheim, and Axelrod (1947-58) would indicate that only the bare beginnings have been made by the sociology of knowledge in measuring distortions in the processes of learning and belief.

Since the sociology of knowledge has as its central task the discovery of the social sources of truth, error, and opinion, it must necessarily take into account the functional role of sexual taboos and tolerations in the advancement of knowledge. Freud (1930) was correct in pointing out that the solution of primary economic needs, and the consequent freeing of a portion of society from a condition of pure scarcity, led to the production of distinctive psychic types which played a critical role in the growth of science, ideology and religion. It is no less true that with leisure we have the justification of a form of society in which class distinctions are sanctioned. And one role of the classic State has been to justify, to rationalize, the bifurcation of society into leisure groups and laboring groups. This then, may be the genesis of ideological thinking—a type of thought driven by private economic or sexual motivations formed by membership in social classes, religious institutions, and cultural groups.

Large-scale consequences flow from a recognition of the psycho-

logical dimension in ideological formations. This may be illustrated at a primary level by an application of Freudian categories
of the sub-conscious. The extent to which the Id is the psychic
reflection of instinctual biological patterns moving counter to established cultural tolerances, the degree to which the Ego and
Superego reflect a conformist impulse of the personality to ac-
quiesce in social domination, are matters which the neo-Freudians
have been concerned with for some time. And it is incumbent
upon sociologists of knowledge to deepen these discussions. It
might begin by asking the extent to which the self-consciousness
of sub-conscious factors in behaviour condition and effect the sexual behaviour of people. Kardiner's work along this path (1949)
has been particularly useful.

For the sociology of knowledge, psychological information presents a crucial challenge concerning the types of ideological rationalizations made by individuals and cultures to protect various
sorts of interests. It raises questions as to the most susceptible
type of psychological attitude for the production of scientific
work. If it is the case that certain types of pathological deformi-
ties may enhance, rather than retard artistic growth, may not the
same situation hold in the discovery of scientific laws? Certainly,
what Freud says of the relation of the poet to day-dreaming
(1908) is not qualitatively different from what Poincaré describes
as the institutional basis of mathematical creation (1913). The
evidence of psychiatry no longer permits a casual taking for
granted of the contradiction between scientific and ideological
production. That they differ is *prima facie* clear. But so too do
artistic and mathematical creation differ from neurosis. The point
is to show, first, how they differ; and second, how they penetrate
each other. Thus it is clear that the very existence of psychoanalysis has made possible the raising of new questions for the sociology of knowledge—questions which it can ignore only at its
own peril by a return to sterile "sociologism."

What has been noted in this survey is the relative intercon-
nectedness of the social sciences, particularly those which have as
a primary concern the source of knowledge in socio-economic and
political institutions. This interchange is crucial if a greater
degree of exactness is to be gained. As Lenzen (1954, 1955) has

indicated, the tasks of the social sciences are complicated by the absence of controlled experimentation in the analytic situation. Since every social event is complex, this places a greater methodological strain on the social sciences than would otherwise be the case. Nonetheless, precisely because of the complex levels involved in social analysis, the collaboration of social sciences with one another must be a real functional union and no mere juxtaposition of performances. (Cf. Germani, 1955b; and Gittler, 1940.)

An integrated approach to the sociology of knowledge involves an initial belief in the capacity of science to comprehend and solve the problem of value in social theory. Even if we were to accept the notion that no ontic demonstration of the superiority of one axiomatic system over another can be adequately framed, this is not sufficient reason to reject scientific methodology. It is in the consequences of science, in the rational determination of future events, that we measure the superiority of science over intuition, rationality over irrationality.

In viewing the social determinants of knowledge as a problem rather than as a fact, the sociology of knowledge offers a distinct dimension for social research. At the first level, it separates factual, logical and normative statements. At the second level, it provides an analysis of the social basis of mental production as well as the deviants in thought. At the third level, the sociology of knowledge separates the various ideological and non-ideological elements in the formation of any given science. At each of these three levels, what is involved is an intimate concern with both the social system and with the sciences dealing with the social system. Thus, knowledge is both the object of study and the ultimate purpose of the sociology of knowledge.

The sociology of knowledge does not simply utilize contributions from the other social sciences. At the core of the discipline is its efforts to explain the ideological components of each social science as a factor in mental production. One importance of a sociology of knowledge is that it offers a way of explaining sociology as a discipline and sociologists as men. Neurath (1944), in discussing the possibilities of a sociology of sociology, noted that "as long as we cannot classify the sociological hypotheses, we can hardly expect great success in finding correlations among sociological hypotheses and other social items." That a functional sociology can classify itself is no more unusual than a photographic camera taking pictures of itself by means of a mirror.

A deplorable element in the history of the social sciences has been the use of pseudo-scientific language to promote narrow political interests and credos. Authority and tenacity, Peirce's two options to a scientific methodology, have grown powerful—but not as independent methods as Peirce forecasted. Rather, they come disguised in racial or regional garb, as sciences of a higher type. The suppression of social science rarely proceeds candidly in our sophistical age. Philistinism comes as philanthropy, or it may even show up as a defense of orthodox science against new-fangled revisions. Doctrinal conformity becomes the hallmark of validating propositions. Ideas are seen as true to the degree to which they faithfully represent entrenched interests. Revisionism becomes a term of opprobrium. This is the standard form of a "scientific" ideology. The antiseptic role performed by the sociology of knowledge can thus best be illustrated by reference to a critical exposition of those tendencies in the social sciences we have already briefly explored.

To start with, it could be said of Veblen and Weber that their respective emphasis on the consuming aspects of economy, rather than on production as such, represented the shifting interests of capitalism more than the shifts in social structure as such. The products of a machine technology, and not technology itself, becomes central. And with Keynes, the circulation of money becomes more important than the real values money represents. The solution of problems in mass production generated problems in ways of stimulating mass consumption. Marketing, distribution, retailing, advertising, all become central in value as well as fact. In part, Veblen and Weber were unconsciously responding to the requirements and aims of an industrial private enterprise economy. The extent to which their respective visions of socialism was a challenge to large-scale industrialism from the perspective of a politically disengaged intelligentsia can be gauged by the emphasis they give to issues which are unique to an advanced capitalism, where social fluidity and mobility is the rule and not the exception. (Cf. Gottlieb, 1953.)

The now dominant emphasis in political science likewise reflects a new social context. Questions of power distribution rather than those touching on the genesis of power become central. The clearest break with the classical tradition in political theory was made earlier in the century by Michels, Pareto and Mosca, and has been pursued avidly since. It might be asked to what degree this reflects a shift in the actual relationship of polity to economy, or is simply a change in the vocabulary of social science from the more clearly etched area of economic controls and sources of power to the ambiguous and value-beholden issues of political domination and status striving.

It may be the case that actual relations between the economic and political forces have altered in the modern world, but how does this entail the notion that centralized State authority displaces the fundamental role of the economic system? Granting that in a free market of operation, economic laws work themselves out mysteriously, to what extent does the absence of a laisserfaire situation recast the position of State coercion in the economic regulation and distribution? Certainly the operation of the economies by the State under Fascism and National Socialism, not to mention the increased policy-making role of the State in the United States and the Soviet Union offers serious food for study, without seeking refuge in the simplistic language of *realpolitik*. *Wissenssoziologie* might contribute to this by examining how different or how similar analysis of present political systems would be given the differences between a structural-functional approach on one side, and an historical approach on the other. (Cf. Neumann, 1957; Michels, 1927.)

Assuredly, the power thesis of political scientists are partially an unconscious response to genuine changes in the relation of economy to polity. But just as clearly, the power thesis performs an ideological function by focusing exclusively on who gets what, rather than upon the more pregnant (and difficult) theme of who gets what under what socio-economic conditions. The perspective of pure egoism in political theory, the return to Bentham's method of counting heads and purses, underlies a great deal of speculation in the area. The orientation towards egoism and the abstract union of egos in civil society is part and parcel of the traditional defense of capitalism as an economic and political system. The refinement of utilitarianism, of notions of self interest and the self regulation of monetary systems, by Galbraith (1958), is perhaps one of the most notable elements in the ideological arsenal of advocates of the power theory.

Nor can psychoanalysis escape the consequences of its origins in the petty bourgeois atmosphere of *fin de siècle* Vienna. As Riesman (1954) reminds us, this is a fact quite apart from the personal privations suffered by the founders of psychoanalysis. "Freud knew penury as a youth—financial needs drove him out of the laboratory and into practice—but it was still the penury of the rising student, not of the destitute proletariat. He assumed that the individualistic motives of getting on in the world, the desires of fame and success, were perfectly 'natural'; it did not occur to him that they might be culturally stimulated or produced, let alone that they might be, in themselves, neurotic drives."

The social circumstances of the patients, no less than of the analysts, were clearly enveloped by middle class standards of conduct. The acrimonious claims of catholic and socialist theorists that psychoanalysis was framed as a secular response to bourgeois religious and moral needs is not without solid support. The trend of analysis reflects a distinctly individualist concern with inner motivational factors such as infantile experiences that tends to suppress the social aspects of mental disorder. Analysis brought about bifurcations in the theory of personality. The mind was separated from the brain, psychiatry separated from neurology, and sexuality separated from sociality. The reintroduction of abstract polarizations of self and society, *Eros* and *Thanatos*, pleasure and pain, was made without apparent awareness that psychoanalysis in this way merely brought into play theories which the classic philosophers had discarded.

The lasting importance of Freud's later writings was his realization that an ambiguity resided in an individualist treatment of what is essentially a mass problem, i.e., the neurotic personality. The chief currents of psychoanalysis, however, continue to offer subjective solutions to social ailments. Thus it rarely comes to grips with the relation of labor, leisure and sexuality. Were the psychoanalytic movement not so bound by middle class clientele and values, it might ask the degree to which the solution of technological problems (and the resultant reduction in types and length of work) tends to maximize rather than alleviate forms of neurosis. Unfortunately, the dominant trends in psychoanalysis, with such notable exceptions as the work in the twenties of Reich (1925, 1946), Fenichel (1927), and Freud (1917), tend to ask the more trivial question of how a repressed individual can adjust to the social requirements of a repressive society.

F. Riessman and Miller (1959) have pointed out that this type of question, most frequently asked by the neo-Freudians, emphasizes the continuity or similarity between neurosis and normality. Since all people suffer from isolation, hostility, search for acceptance and affection, only a quantitative distinction could be made between mental sickness and health (Brill, 1949:22-23). And through the use of such phrases as the "sick society" and the "sane society," neo-Freudianism tended to assume a disguised moral stance, conducive to the ideological needs of the leisured portion of society rather than the medical needs of the mentally sick and retarded. The notion of character neurosis in contrast to symptom neurosis was developed to reinforce a "moral" approach to mental illness. (Cf. Horney, 1937.)

Typical of psychonanalysis as a new ideology is the work of Fromm (1941, 1947, 1955). Underlying Fromm's humanistic psychoanalysis is a pragmatic ideology. Methods for fixing belief replace the causal analysis of how beliefs are sifted and selected. Methods of fixing belief are carefully expounded: authority, destruction and self-destruction, automatic conformity, are considered the principal mode of the escape from freedom. As in Peirce, who wrote eighty years earlier, the machinery of social domination used to impose its will over people is reversed. As Marcuse (1955) and Brown (1959) indicate, in Fromm, mechanisms of oppression are transformed into mechanisms of personal evasion. By subjectivizing the relation between repression and belief, while yet honestly seeking a humanistic alternative to barbarism, Fromm turns psychoanalysis into social adjustment.

Self-actualization and introspective insight, concepts peculiarly suited to the ethos of an educated middle class, becomes the dominant motif. Fromm's "communitarian socialism" is not so much a return to freedom as it is a verbal substitute for freedom through the longing after utopia. His assumption that coercion is necessarily undemocratic ignores the concrete goals which coercion strives to attain.

Man does not escape from freedom, since the nature of freedom is itself defined by the root factors of social coercion, toleration and liberty (in the form of mobility, motility, security, etc.). Integration of the personality into polity, and not emancipation of the private person from the manifold elements in public repression, is what underlies the neo-Freudian thought of Brill, Horney and Sullivan. As Rieff recently commented (1959: 338), "the combination of a repressive political order with a permissive moral order is not unheard of in human history. And indeed, today's automatic political repressions parody the Freudian description of *private* repressive culture." The analyst is himself in need of *outside* analysis, just as the nineteenth century noted that the Enlightenment educator was himself in need of outside education. And the kind of analysis most needed at present is sociological.

The concepts of the "Superego" and the "Censor" are in some part a microscopic representation of the formal categories of political economy. Repression is the internalization of the notion of oppression. If this is so, what is the position of psychoanalysis on the resolution of repression? Similarly, if adjustment psychology is related to social attitudes of conformity, in what way is it possible for it to maintain its posture of value neutrality? Given the unwritten compact of the analyst with his society, to what degree can psychoanalysis move from ideological prescription to scientific description? The fact that such issues can be raised is indicative of the conflicting elements that form the matrix of present-day psychoanalytic doctrine.

Nor can the sociology of knowledge be less critical with respect to its own social limits. The type of solution offered by Mannheim to the pendulum of ideology (controlling interests) and utopia (outside interests), is no less a distended reproduction of middle class elitist values than are to be found elsewhere in the social science spectrum. Indeed, the notion of the socially unbound intellectual involves a special interest attitude of the thinker *vis a vis* the active man. It is the speculative notion of science inherited from Hegelian thought. Mannheim's intellectual is a man who steadily rinses his brain with ideas, but never knows enough to wash his hands with soap. Elitism underscores this position because of the assumption that truth is intrinsically the preserve of only a small, trained section of the populace. Mannheim at least resisted the more obvious implications of elitism; Scheler, to the contrary, never doubted the healing power of a conservative elite.

This faith in the expert reveals a more profound shortcoming in the work of Mannheim and Scheler. For despite the differences between the two on the worth of pragmatism, Marxism and liberalism, they shared the view that a sociology of knowledge is a study of the social roots of errors. Granted the assumption that the interests of a particular social force necessarily represents an ideological position, no non-ideological (social scientific) standpoint can be developed without a transcendental force—in Mannheim's case, the intellectual, in Scheler's case, the theologian. To be engaged in the main currents of political or social life is to be committed to an ideology, at least operationally. To be ideologically bound is to surrender the quest for truth. Thus, in Mannheim's reasoning in particular, the search for social truth requires a disengagement from every day life. Such a view is not so much a prescription for the necessary preconditions for attaining true knowledge, as it is an unintentional description of the position of scholarship in western society. The functioning divisions between head and hand, theory and action, are not viewed as special features of industrial society, but as the general feature of scientific knowledge. (Cf. Lukacs, 1953: ch. VI, pt. 5.)

A sociology of science must begin by recognizing the connection of scientific knowledge to the material functions of society as a whole. The inter-subjective method of verification precludes any possibility that science is restrictive along occupational lines. Certain social systems do retard scientific advancement, but this carries no implication that science as such is open to one social class or ethnic group and closed to the rest of society. In refining the social roots of error, the sociology of knowledge can help define the necessary conditions for the discovery of social truths. In this enterprise those sharing in the scientific attitude can make substantial contributions; not because the social scientist or the natural scientist is liberated from class, religious or national convictions or conventions, but because science has the capacity to make these factors part of its analytic calculations. (Cf. Reichenbach, 1951; Cohen, 1954; DeGré, 1955).

Important as it is to calculate the quantity of distortion resulting from human intervention in subjects like microphysics, it is still more urgently required in social scence, where intervention of distortions from human concerns is directly related to prediction. The scientific study of values and norms is therefore a direct complement to the formation of a sociology of knowledge. Any contrary assumption, any view which holds the ultimately capricious nature of moral decision, would make the task of the sociology of knowledge extremely difficult if not impossible. The development of a clear set of hypotheses for explaining how moral decisions are made has been stymied for the most part by the logical positivist assertion that moral statements are emotive rather than denotative. In offering a distinction between ethics (the science of moral judgments) and morals (the selection of a goal itself), positivism made a huge step forward in the study of moral propositions. Unfortunately, in accepting the dualism between ethics and morals as final, and in dealing analytically only with the former, the empirical status of moral judgment was left undefined and unrefined. (Cf. Horowitz, 1958a.) The reciprocity of ethical theory and the sociology of knowledge is rooted in the common desire to distinguish the basis for rationally arriving at moral decisions, from the emotive, interest-bound elements unconsciously at work. An ethical theory rooted in social science methodology is no guarantee that moral traditions will topple, only that we will have more informed knowledge of how moral decisions are socially arrived at and sanctioned. (Cf. Edel, 1955, 1956b; Mandelbaum, 1955; Ginsberg, 1948.)

The unity of the social sciences is not a device for turning back to pure empiricism, for a formalistic analysis lacking in prescriptive and directional value. It is a search for the forms through which it might be possible to realize a scientific theory of ethics without resorting to a carving up of the moral universe into phenomenal and noumenal elements. The function of the sociology of knowledge in this joint social and philosophical enterprise is to describe the role of social-political interests in the determination of moral choices; and thus make decision-making itself more conscious and rational.

Chapter VII

Social Knowledge and Ideological Configurations

In THE language of social research, few words have proven as controversial and yet as influential as "ideology." Marx (1846) gave the word its first modern definition by employing it as part of a general theory of the production and reproduction of ideas. However, the initial use of the word ideology must be ascribed to the French philosopher, Destutt de Tracy (1801). Unlike Marx, de Tracy thought of ideology as a synonym for broad scientific ideas and ideals, and not as a special form of knowledge. And while there are still those who employ ideology in this way, its real value to a sociology of knowledge begins when ideology is differentiated from other forms of knowledge, i.e., scientific, poetic, religious. (Cf. Barth, 1945: ch. 1.)

Ideology has increasingly been used to signify a mediating point in the spectrum of human knowledge. Thus ideology is (a) an amalgamation of true and false consciousness: (b) a justification for either revolutionary or reactionary interests and attitudes in political life; (c) a rationalization of irrational forms of social and psychological motivation. In short, ideology expresses that point in social knowledge at which interests connect up to a picture of reality.

An ideology involves a series of ideas related to definite social ambitions. It is a *special* series of ideas—neither the magical, religious symbols which linked all primitive men to their natural common protagonists, nor the scientific ideas which now focus the energies of men in the same struggle against nature's vicissitudes. The universality of magic, science and religion stems precisely from the common task of capturing from nature the secrets of material abundance. Ideology functions neither as a religious nor a scientific formulator. The reverse is more often the case. It operates as a social justification or criticism of the stage men have reached in the unbalanced relation between scarcity and abundance.*

An ideology, in so far as its purpose is to convince, and this implies the presence of a coercive element, bases its appeal upon a circle or class of people who have social aims in common. But both religion and science appeal to "everyone," to the undifferentiated mass in the social world. In contradistinction to ideology, science and religion strive for a universal validation of their claims (which is not to be confused with universal comprehensibility). And universal validity, for science derived through experience and for religion derived through revelation, must be capable of being made separate from the personality of the knower. It is precisely this which marks ideology as distinct, since it can never be divorced from the personality, i.e., the interests, of the knower, or from the collective class authority which supports an ideology. There are no grounds for viewing an ideology as a vast continuum infusing all forms and styles of knowledge. It is furthermore unwarranted to declare investigation of the objective functioning of an ideological system invalid on the grounds that the investigator too has an ideology. Since an ideology has defined limits, the real question of analysis shifts from how one can "escape" his ideology, to a comparative analysis of ideological systems in the first instance, and a comparison of ideologies with other forms of knowledge in the second instance.

We must first consider the type of ideas which comprise an ideological system. In the first place, no ideology reflects the total range of social interests. Ideological attitudes are perspectivally limited by the concrete interests of the special group, and no less by the interpersonal relations within the group.

---

* The social basis of religious ideas is a topic having a vast literature unto itself. Although it does not directly enter into our analysis, the works of Malinowski (1948), Eliade (1958), Radin (1953), Durkheim (1912), Engels (1894), Weber (1904), Cassirer (1946), and Honigsheim (1958) should be consulted for information on the sociology of religion and its bearing on knowledge in general. In this connection, the recent compilation by J. Milton Yinger (1957) can be profitably consulted.

False consciousness, by which we mean such things as magic, mystery-cults and mythology, has a root connection to true consciousness, which is employed as equivalent to the claims of science. While ideology asserts the universality of its claims also, it does so from the vantage point of a given social stratum with an economic-political stake either in preserving or liquidating established socio-political relations. It is thus the condition of existence of this given social stratum which is the ultimate source of an ideology, rather than real or imagined social needs in general. ?

If there is a need to be emphatic about treating ideology as something apart from a system of universal validation, there is equal need to deal with ideology as a social fact and not simply a private utterance. Durkheim correctly insisted upon treating social facts as things, as social events in themselves distinct from the consciously formed representation of them in the mind. (Cf. Durkheim, 1895: ch. 2.) Now Durkheim went a step further in considering philosophy and morality as having a two-fold subjective and objective character; in consequence of which the sociologist can illumine these fields by treating even philosophic and moral statements as things. (Cf. Durkheim, 1924: ch. 2.) There is every reason to assume that, by extension, once we accept the principle that both facts and ideas can be treated as things for scientific investigation (given the proviso that these facts and ideas are socially held and have a temporal duration of use), the same approach holds for the scientific study of ideologies.

I propose to take up the question of ideology as that which is over and above any individual proponent or any private whim. Ideology is, from the point of view of the sociology of knowledge, the investigation of the social uses of ideas for the purpose of convincing or coercing men into actions having ultimate political and economic consequences. While such a definition is clearly more ambitious than that given earlier in the chapter, it does fuller justice to the practical, goal-directed element in the relation of interests to an image of reality. Indeed, when Durkheim's "moral authority of the collective" is considered as an ideology, it raises distinctly sociological questions not of the truth of moral propositions, but of their effectiveness in the preservation of this collective authority. The sociology of knowledge has thus a double problem on its hands: (a) to examine the political use value of an ideological configuration; and (b) to examine the truth content of any given ideology.

In order to clarify my use of the term ideology, it will be helpful to examine some other, more classical uses of ideology. While there are obvious overlapping points, it should be noted that all five of the definitions given below (and which I reject) tend to consider ideology as "total," as defining knowledge as a whole, rather than as a special form of knowledge with a unique social role.

To view ideology as a total distortion in our general orientation, as distinct from particular problems, as Mannheim (1929, 1935) does, is to miss the point that science, poetry, mythology, no less than ideology, involve a "general will" as well as particular wills. This being the case, it is not possible to consider ideology as simply the general ideas of a social class or of society as a whole. Mannheim's difficulty is that he tended to equate the "interest bound" and the obscuring of real social conditions by a Jungian "collective unconscious," with any false notions about nature and society. The equation of ideology with false consciousness led to a deterioration in the quality of his examination of such phenomena as magic and theology. Once a more modest approach to the limits of ideology is taken, we need not make the equation of "total ideology" to "total distortions"—an equation whose use in social science is dubious on empirical as well as logical grounds.

Other kinds of problems arise from an earlier view of ideology, that of Lenin (1908). He considers ideology as a simple quantitative distinction in ideas. Ideology is said to contain a range of ideas from false notions of the ruling class to the true notions of the revolutionary class. On Lenin's premises, ideology is reduced to a heuristic principle for regulating theory. He thus finds no difficulty in employing terms like "scientific ideology" and "religious ideology." With Lenin, ideology no longer was a special relation of ideas to material institutions as it was in Marx. Political alliance replaces class affiliation as the touchstone for estimating ideologies. Admittedly, Lenin was dealing with a political context requiring immediate ideological choices. He was confronted with a situation demanding a wholesale commitment to certain policies on the part of an elite and its following. In this context, Lenin contributed to a wide realization that oppressed and oppressor cannot automatically transcend ideological boundaries; that ideology is indeed a barrier to be passed. Thus a revolutionary conflict, in so far as it engages the mental energies of the combatants, is no intellectual idyll, but rather a hard fought struggle between ideologies. What Lenin did not understand, and what was already apparent to the psychological school of Michels, Sorel, and Pareto, is that ideology first and foremost functions symbolically to galvanize men into action. Ideology contains an irrational element without which it could serve no moral or political end, and this end exists quite apart from the intrinsic needs of a scientific sociology. (Cf. Barzun, 1941.)

This view of ideology as only quantitatively differentiated from other forms of knowledge, i.e., ideology as continuous and contiguous with science, re-appears in the work of Sorokin (1951: ch. 11.) Here, as with Lenin, we find the terms "scientific" and "religious" ideology. But unlike either his Russian nemesis, or the Italian psychological school, Sorokin sees in ideology only "the totality of meanings, values, and norms" without the fulfillment of these norms through institutional or revolutionary activities. When Sorokin speaks of "mere ideology" he in effect reduces ideology to talking about things rather than acting on them. Overt action for Sorokin is "behavioral" rather than ideological. Ideology is the incarnation of such behavior in the realm of politics, religion, etc. Sorokin sees the "total empirical culture" of a person or group as made up of three cultural levels: ideological, behavioral and material. (Cf. Sorokin, 1947: ch. 17.) In this way, ideology is distinguished from both the material culture and from the sphere of social action. The difficulty in Sorokin's view is that: (a) ideology is separated from its very *raison d'être*, a stimulant to action; and (b) ideology becomes another word for talking about and justifying things, without any essential properties of its own. This creates the basis for a more serious criticism of Sorokin's vision of the total ideology. It is deprived of any sociological status, since one may construct "private ideologies" no less than "public ideologies." As soon as ideology is so subjectivized, i.e., transformed into a psychological category, it loses its operational value in the study of socially conditioned elements in thought. Sorokin moved close to the Augustinian division of mankind into sensate, idealist, and fideist Beings. And as Speier (1952: ch. 16) has observed, this led Sorokin closer to a rigid moral catechism than to a general theory of the social roots of knowledge—what he was ostensibly searching for. The conversion by Sorokin of these "Augustinian" types into typical culture-stages (and hence as truly ideological) only reinforced his identification of religion and ideology.

Scheler, whose philosophical inspiration was more from Kant than either Hegel or Augustine, nonetheless (and like Dilthey) erects an approach to ideology that is quantitative and fails to limit its range of operations. All ideas, myths, legends, science, religion, are said to contain ideological elements. (Cf. Scheler, 1926, 1928.) Indeed, it is hard to see where ideology is anything but a given *Weltanschauung* localized in historical space. Where Scheler is unique is in ascribing to the realm of philosophic knowledge the same importance as one might ascribe to social or economic institutions. But Scheler wished to avoid relativizing the phenomenal world. He attempted an escape from relativism by relating the possession of knowledge to the possession of political power. The elite couples possession of knowledge with responsibility for society as a whole. Philosophy becomes a built-in mechanism for adjusting the interests of the elite to the truths of the universe. Scheler's critique of Marxism and pragmatism revolved about their inability to account for the existence of truths in social living, i.e., their shared insistence that the realm of class or cash interests is the whole reality.

Scheler's own "escape" from relativism involved a transcendental theory of ideology. The elite is propelled by an ethical perspective that is nourished, but not exhausted, by material events (1926:48). Scheler attempted a fusion between historical relativism and a phenomenalist counter-relativism by agreeing with the former that history explains, and is explained by, social relations; and by agreeing with the latter that the validation of belief is a matter of perception rather than of history. Thus unlike Mannheim, the determination of social ideas is not equated to the logical truth of ideas. But Scheler's position only consecrates a metaphysical dualism no less dogmatic than the relativism it seeks to overcome. By carving reality into existence and essence, ideologically conditioned and metaphysically unconditioned, Scheler succeeds only in assuring religion an exemption from sociological analysis (1927:I:483-91). His view does not actually promote investigation of the social determination of ideas, which was the original intent, since certain types of ideas are *apriori* ruled out of social causation. The long-range consequence of Scheler's outlook is to make of ideology a secular religion, lacking in the timeless truths of revealed religion. The empirical study of ideology might begin with Scheler's effort to overcome the dissolution of truth into the historical flux, but it could not get far without overcoming his own dissolution of history into timeless categories.

The last type of view to be considered, and probably that conception of ideology most popularly expounded, is that an ideology is simply a profane and fanatical religion. This morally "reprehensible" theory of ideology is ably presented by Toynbee (1956). He seems particularly fond of the "common-sense" belief that ideology is a "secular inheritance of religious fanaticism." But here too we are confronted with a purely quantitative equation of ideology with ideas in general. Toynbee's position, which oddly enough, is an extension of Scheler's dualism, has the further deficit of yielding a moral criterion of fanaticism in place of an analysis of the genesis and function of ideology in social existence. Toynbee ignores the possibility of an ideology being no less ideological if it propagates gentle, Christian ideas of universal happiness under the rule of common law, than if it advocates open defiance of the *status quo*. To view either Locke's or Mill's concept of democracy as being free of ideological determinants, and Marx' concept of democracy as purely ideological, is not to explain the meaning of ideology, but rather to convert the word itself into a part of the struggle for the minds of men. (Cf. Horowitz, Joynt, 1958.)

These inherited views of ideology examined, it might be useful to see how, and in what ways, ideology differs from religion and science; and from that point, go on to a consideration of possible ideological configurations.

The evolution of consciousness took clear form in efforts to master the physical universe through the mechanisms of magic, ritual, myth and religion, and other types of "pre-philosophy." The production of these ideas, irrespective of their explanatory worth, is a social production. It is an effort undertaken by society as a whole to solve outstanding problems confronting man as a whole. But with, and through, this effort to define the structure of reality by appeals to the unknown, there also arises the genesis of the scientific attitude. As Radin (1927, 1936) has pointed out, the content of magic is as much an appeal to empirical description and a logical ordering of known events, as it is faith in the forces of the unknown. Magic and religion, the witch-doctor and the priest, were leading members in the community precisely because they did possess real knowledge and logical solutions to problems as disparate as building boats and healing the sick.

A major difficulty in Levy-Bruhl's (1922) work is that the division of human types into logical and pre-logical exhibits a twentieth century mind as the logical norm, and ignores the problem of logic as satisfying the functional needs of a social system. To ignore the naturalistic element in primitive religion leads to the false view of science as a special invention of the Greek mind. And perhaps even Heraklitos would have to be classed as a primitive deviant since he did not believe in the law of contradition. What Levy-Bruhl did not grasp, and what is essential if we are to gain an understanding of the special features of ideology, is that false consciousness is inextricably committed to true consciousness in two distinct ways: they share a common socialized base, and they both make explanations and predictions. In this connection it should be mentioned that neither scientific laws nor religious systems vanish with each change in the structure of polity or economy. This is not to say that they are unaffected by such changes, but they are affected in terms of acceleration and retardation. Ideology, on the other hand, which also *claims* universal truth, is directly subject to obsolescence through historical change. It emerges or is destroyed as that social class which advocates it emerges or is destroyed.

A cardinal feature in Marx' (1846) analysis of the problem of ideology was his location of the source of ideology, not in society as a whole but in the operations of that portion of society consecrated as the State. The State becomes the guarantor of social stability between economic units divided as to function and relation to one another. The State is said to be in *fact* the coercive arm of one social force against the rest of society. But in *theory* the State offers itself as guardian of the social interests and mores. Reinforcing this dichotomy between the real and imagined role of the State, a dichotomy which is at the core a struggle for political domination, Marx located the source of ideology in class interests, rather than in the interest of men as a whole.

In the "contradiction between the interest of the individual and that of the community, the latter takes an independent form as the *State,* divorced from the real interests of individual and community, and at the same time as an illusory communal life." Precisely this separation of the individual from the communal is disguised by the ideology. The attempt to maintain this disguise, through propaganda, promises, and even coercion, leads to a special situation in the area of social thought. "The ideas of the ruling class are in every epoch the ruling ideas, that is, the class which is the ruling material force of society, is at the same time its ruling intellectual force." While this would account for the production of the dominant ideology, we are still left, in Marx' writings, without an answer to the question of how counter-ideologies are produced. Indeed, Marx (1847:140-41) seems to identify the counter-ideology of the proletariat with general scientific truth. Which is to say that Marx identifies what is socially exploited with what is scientifically correct.

A more adequate explanation of how counter-ideologies are produced would have to start from the premise that new ideologies expressing changes in material relations are no less hinged to power relations than older forms of intellectual rationalization. The counter-ideology poses issues as a general abolition of the old in the name of the common good, in roughly the same way as the dominant State ideology represents itself as the best or even only defense of the same common good. Therefore the production of counter-ideologies is in itself not necessarily a step toward a more scientific appraisal of social realities, anymore than the coercive factor in the dominant State ideology is proof of a theory of Divine Rights. Every ideology and counter-ideology serves as a system of disguises and promises justifying coercive power. Whatever the ratio of scientific and unscientific elements in the ideological conscience, the existence of *both* elements is pre-requisite for establishing a functioning ideology.

The superiority of one ideology over another depends on the type of values prized and praised by the group. The basic variable may be the need for an heroic elite to maintain social progress; in that case, an ideology which readily arouses and sustains the warrior instincts might be judged best. Those who place a supreme value on science, will judge that ideology best which advocates high decision making roles for scientists. If the chief aim of the group is radical social and economic change, the tendency will be to promote an ideology holding out hope for increased planning, subsidization for key industries, and guaranteed pensions and salaries. What binds ideologies is a common need to present social problems in terms of moral perspectives.

Whatever the ratio of descriptive and prescriptive elements in an ideology, it is clearly a different qualitative entity than either religion or science. To speak of a "scientific" ideology is a contradiction in fact as well as logic. It indicates an increase of sophistication on the part of the possessors of political power, not the transformation of ideology into science. The price of this historicism is the displacement of social science as an instrument for explaining the operative threads in human society. Politically, the concept of ideology is cemented to social practice. This alone would make the notion of a scientific ideology suspect.

Socialist politics offers good evidence for rejecting the idea of scientific ideology. Revolutionary socialism employs this notion to prove that the theory and practice of the revolutionary party exhausts the possibilities of social science. Thus any social science not attached to directly political ends becomes heretical. The dogma of the unity of theory and practice, upon which such a "scientific" ideology rests, assumes as true what has to be proved in every situation, i.e., that useful social activities require a corresponding theoretical system. Nor can reform socialism assume that its notion of the rational, evolutionary road to economic reconstruction escapes the dilemmas of more activist ideologies. The "scientific" ideology of West European socialism is precisely a case of the incompatibility of the two terms. Official socialism transformed itself from a movement for political emancipation into one of immediate economic amelioration. Its politics became indistinguishable from other political parties in aims and structure. But this dissolution of politics into legality is, no less, the suppression of counter-ideology. It is an implicit acceptance of the criteria for legitimacy set forth by the dominant ideology. The complete reform doctrine is an acquiescence in the criteria set forth by the dominant ideological configuration—which are criteria not necessarily shared by a mature sociology. The rational, scientific ideology (whatever variety it takes) can therefore become the most thorough acquiescence in the *status-quo.*

Ideology is not, however, simply a rationalization of contending social forces, but more important, a genuine representation of the irrational ambitions and drives of such forces. The evidence would indicate that the promotion of action requires appeals to non-verifiable moral postulates. (Cf. Bergmann, 1951; Dantzig, 1951; Nettler, 1957.) Within existing social patterns exhibiting conflicting political and economic forces, the irrationality of State power insinuates itself upon civil society as universal law. The possible success of a counter-ideology depends upon the material force of its claim to upset the claims to universality of the dominant ideology. The counter-ideology can also maintain its ability to get results. Indeed, one of its appeals is usually its capacity to yield results efficiently and with a minimum of human suffering.

Anticipating the next chapter somewhat, we may say that the movement of the ideological into the utopian is the concretization of thought in action. Utopianism is not a passive concept. The ideological goal once conceived, must be executed in practice. Utopianism forms the core of a counter-ideology, becoming the dream of the future with which to smash present practices. The demand for total action requires a commitment to future ideals far and above tentative, reform demands. Immediate demands can satisfactorily be made and resolved within an ideological system. They do not involve the same "ultimate" claims as does a counter-ideology. The partial or complete realization of the heavenly city of Plato, Augustine, More or Rousseau, calls into being a total struggle between ideology and counter-ideology. The quest for utopia creates the spiritual condition for a total struggle between the contending economic and political forces.

In this struggle between a State ideology and utopian counter-ideologies, what is the place of the "rational" man? To personalize the problem somewhat, let us use the "Hamlet Paradox" first raised by Goethe and recently reproduced by Reichenbach (1951). Hamlet was that heroic literary figure who represented a thoroughly rational man, but emotionally refined to such a degree that he was unable to resolve the duality of knowledge and action. The consequence of Hamlet's demand for rational certitude was the inhibition of action. Knowledge of alternative possibilities created the seeds of disintegration by generating quietude in the face of existing evils. In this rational (but not necessarily scientific) individual, ideology might have functioned as a cathartic agent to eliminate indecision, if not imprecision. The point is not whether ideology is good or evil, but its demonstrated capacity to organize and galvanize all forms of action, good and evil, scientific and otherwise. (Cf. Schumpeter, 1949.) The rational man may be held up as the ideal toward which the human race ought to strive, but this should not blur the fact that this very value of reason is itself measured by the extent to which science allows for social advancement. The ethic of abundance underlies the ends of the scientific revolution as assuredly as the older ethic of thrift underlay the ends of the capitalist revolution.

This approach carries no implication that science *per se* makes men incapable of decisive action. It is to say that the aims of science can and are embodied by certain ideologies in which the ultimate value is social abundance. So stated, there is no need to urge the creation of a behavioral science elite for the purpose of combatting the ideologists. Such a Mannheim type of position merely recreates the notion of the double truth which has plagued intellectual history from the outset. In the name of science, it perniciously gives rise to a separation of truth-dispensers and truth-seekers—the very thing which the sociology of knowledge sets out to overcome. The social sciences can measure and evaluate the mechanisms at the disposal of human beings in the effort of society to realize its most cherished ambitions. But until such ambitions are, in fact, realized, science cannot consider itself a guaranteed substitute for ideology. Counter-ideologies in particular may help restructure human ideals for the purpose of promoting a social force as powerful, if not more so, than the ideological solidarity presented by the State agencies. In such an historical imbalance of social classes, it would be folly to suggest that an ideological temper is necessarily immoral or unscientific.

In sum, ideology never can exist apart from its opposite, counter-ideology. Both are a response to the division of man in economy, and no less, a consequence of political concentration of power in elites. For an ideological system is not simply a lever in the promotion of political action, but an instrument offering ideals and alternatives to an unsatisfactory or partially satisfactory social system. The role of science in this connection is to distinguish empirical from ideological claims, not to adopt a messianic attitude toward the former and a missionary attitude toward saving us from the latter.

Chapter VIII

The Structure of Utopianism

THE study of utopianism can be made from a number of perspectives: investigation of utopian communities of the past, analysis of the literary remains of famous utopists of past ages, or the isolation of utopianism as a special form of social consciousness. Here, I shall only be concerned with the last mentioned approach. Specifically, the task will be the study of utopian mentality as a special form of an ideological system—which includes the counter-ideologies as well as the dominant State ideology. In his brilliant study of the general and specific characteristics of the utopian conscience, Ruyer (1950) presented an essentially typological and historical accounting. What I shall attempt is an extension of Ruyer's work by reorganizing his materials in terms of what the utopian consciousness has in common with (a) all ideological configurations, (b) only counter-ideologies, and (c) attempts to avoid any ideological commitment.

After the work of More's *Utopia* (1516) and Campanella's *Civitas Solis* (1623), the word utopia came to be identified with an unattainable social perfection. Thus, for the practicing utopians of the nineteenth century like Fourier, Owen and Weitling, the word utopia itself fell into relative disuse even by those dedicated to realizing social perfection on earth. And with Engels (1880), the term utopian was used as an antonym for a scientific and practical conception of society. Thus, from two sides, the utopian came under heavy fire: from conservatives hostile to experimental approaches to new social forms, and revolutionists hostile to experiments which are to take place *within* existing economic and political relations. Utopianism was considered subversive by one side for the implicit critique it carried of extant social forms, and by the other side as subversive of the general aims of a revolutionary party. Thus from a practical political point of view, utopianism expressed a middle-ground between the extremes of social revolution and social conservation; a function quite unlike that performed by an ideological configuration.

Before we turn to our central topic: the relation of utopianism to ideological configurations, let us briefly compare the utopian vision to religion and science considered as systems of thought.

Like religion, utopian thinking has as its starting point an idea of moral perfection from which it tests present realities. Proselytism and prophetism are built into all utopian systems. That is to say the idea of apocalypse is employed to convince people of the inevitability of fulfillment of the utopia, and as a means to gather a force of prophets to announce the approach of judgment-day. The establishment of utopian colonies, like the building of missionary outposts in "heathen" lands, is not considered an end in itself, but rather the initial thrust of the purified future upon the impure present. Utopian systems share with theological systems a closed and total character, what Ruyer calls "the axiological deception." They have the capacity to explain all present events, since they posit the contours of future society, in terms of an agreed upon philosophy of history. This pre-knowledge of future success, sanctioned as it is by an historical *telos*, makes all sacrifices seem trivial. Asceticism becomes transformed from an economic necessity into a moral virtue. Purification of the soul and moral redemption are made easier by an ascetic approach to personal existence. Indeed, a measurable distinction between leaders and followers in both utopian and religious communities is the extent of personal sacrifice on behalf of the general good. While these characteristics do not exhaust the common ground between the two, they do reveal why utopian and religious attitudes often have been closely linked in the practical life.

While it has become fashionable in the literature of social science to call anything religious which contains a worked out philosophy of history, there are certain irreducible differences between utopian and religious mentalities. The most obvious, and perhaps the most important, is that the former places salvation in the material world, while the latter involves a commitment to supernatural sanctions and solutions./ From this follows the humanism of the utopian system of thought, i.e., the elimination of deities and the ritualistic aspects central in the function of a religion. The notion of a symmetrical ordering of society in terms of the general will leaves no place for providential intervention. It is this cumulative "man makes himself" attitude that has tended to make the utopian mentality politically radical; whereas the institutionalization of an other-worldly dependence tends to reinforce the *status quo* by making human ambitions contingent upon divine instruction. But this distinction between utopian radicalism and religious conservatism can by no means be considered anything more than a phase rule, with a large body of exceptions, each of which requires careful empirical examination.

The points of contact between the utopian and scientific mentalities are, I should say, fewer and less pervasive than that of utopianism and religion. That contact which does exist has more to do with the values held in common by science and utopian thought than with the actual functioning of a scientific body of knowledge. Both accept the principle that all worldly events can be determined with some precision given a large enough supply of evidence. The symmetrical features of the social world are held more important than any individual deviations. What is essential to science and utopian thought is not that everything has been explained, or given present inadequacies can be explained, but rather that explanations can be satisfactorily rendered and practical decisions underwritten on the basis of available evidence. Social planning is therefore as much a part of the utopian vision as it has become of the behavioral sciences.

Nonetheless, when we consider social change from a scientific position, we are concerned with the range of existing possibilities. The dogmatic element in utopian orientations reduces the range of possibilities to one, deriving from competing theories of history. The utopian is concerned with the best, the most morally satisfactory relation of fredom to order. It may urge a reorientation of present industrial and political relations, but always as a means to a higher moral end, and not as a value in itself. (Cf.

Bloch, 1946:11-24.) Utopian systems are not so much fashioned to meet outstanding problems of the moment, as they are attempts to supply ultimate moral challenges to the moment. Herein lies the great divide between science and utopian outlooks.

We are now in a position to explore the relation of utopianism and ideological configurations. Their great similarity inheres in the direct connection they have to the specific social and political structures which generate them. Scientific, religious, technological and artistic considerations enter into a utopian system as a by-product of the social order; and unlike any of these considerations, utopia cannot survive the demise of any given social order. Because of this very kinship to ideologies, we must be careful not to blur the contours of where ideology ends and utopia begins.

The utopian conscience involves appeals to a future commonwealth, while often drawing its materials from past societal arrangements. The utopian thus must look in two directions for inspiration: to a past in which human nature is fetishized and assigned qualities of moral perfection held absent in present human relations, and to a mysterious future supposedly made clearer by extrapolating and extending present scientific and technological achievements. The utopia of a Bacon or a Bellamy, like the counter-utopias of Orwell and Huxley, all bear the marks of this double relation to the past and the future in which everything seems to change but "human nature."

The utopian conscience further represents an imaginative resolution of the options provided between ideological systems. (Cf. Freyer, 1928, 1930.) But the utopian is no less bound by sociopolitical interests than the ideological. The differences between them are spatial and temporal, not differences in kinds of explanation or in types of demands made upon adherents. Ideology is the distorted measure of the distance between where man has been in relation to where he stands at present, while utopianism is a false measurement of the distance between where men stand and where they are heading.

The utopian vision and an ideological constellation should be considered co-ordinate rather than identical. More forcefully stated, they represent an essential inversion of each other. Since the search for the perfect commonwealth (utopia) clearly cannot assume that the perfect commonwealth is in essentials identical to the existing State (ideology), they cannot function in the same way even if we assume a common psychological origin of utopia and ideology. The basic equation is between utopia and counter-ideology on one side, and counter-utopia and ideology on the other.

We are compelled to introduce the idea of counter-utopia to account for the specific form in which the dominant State ideology attempts to counter-act the intrinsically optimistic and radical note struck by utopian constructions. The gloomy visions of an Orwell, whatever their truth content, can certainly not function in support of a counter-ideology urging a revolutionary over-hauling of the economic order. Thus, the inverse relationship established (ideology as promoting counter-utopias, and counter-ideologies as promoting utopias) can be viewed as an operational guide in the study of the social determinants of knowledge.

This, is however, but a starting point for empirical research. There is more to social knowledge than the imagined circularities of ideology and utopia.* A commitment to a self-correcting,

---

* In Mannheim's system, nothing exists independent or outside of the ideological and utopian systems. As Marcuse (1929) and von Schelting (1936) indicated, his approach places even science and history in the position of being functionally dependent upon social-political interests. Since the behavioral sciences in particular are held to be subject to such interests, and in Mannheim's view creates the conditions for utopian systems to move beyond such ideological interests, there can be no genuine escape from relativism. But since total relativism obviates the need for the social scientist altogether, Mannheim had to lift this special man of knowledge out of the realm of social involvement. The *freischwebende Intelligenz* is beholden to all classes, and thus mysteriously to no class in particular. There is a hidden premise that the sociologist of knowledge is a manipulator of information rather than a knower of things. The intellectual in general becomes a *deus ex machina* rooting out error without ever having exact criteria of truth. (Cf. Mannheim, 1929: ch. 3, pt. 5.)

Because in an exact sense, Mannheim was unable to separate the role of interests in shaping knowledge from the possibility of knowledge as such, and was further unable to separate the possession of a utopian constellation from the acquisition of scientific statements about society, he became pessimistic as to the worth of reason as such. He projected his private sentiments onto reality when he declared that at the point man "has achieved the highest degree of rational mastery of existence" he will be "left without any ideals" to become a "mere creature of impulses." (Cf. Mannheim, 1929: ch. 2.) If the sociology of knowledge must come to rest on the circle of ideology and utopia, it will prove incapable of offering more than a refinement of the counter-utopian notions of Huxley and Orwell. If the possibility of

scientific method implies an acceptance of an objective stand-point for verification. This does not mean a *diktat* ordering men to carry on investigations in narrow empiricist terms, as if the procedure of counting heads is a genuine escape from social positioning. The sociology of knowledge should be willing to move beyond the dross of its peculiar inheritance and acknowl-edge that social interests are open to objective analysis and can be viewed as part of the materials the behavioral scientist works with.

This position implies that we define ideological constellations and utopian configurations in such a way that they retain an empirical meaning apart from science. Only then can the rela-tions between forms of knowledge be studied without melting them into one another. We might take Pareto's (1916) position into consideration here, and distinguish ideology from science in terms of the rationalizations each make, and distinguish utopia from science in terms of the place assigned to moral and meta-physical prescriptiveness. But whatever our distinctions, some account must be made in terms of the different levels of meaning at which the various branches of knowledge operate. In the following examination of three fundamental forms of the utopian vision, I hope to make clear not only the relation of these types of utopianism to ideology, but do so in such a way as to make clear the differences between all utopian configurations and the scientific approach to social problems.

As we have noted, an essential aspect in the utopian conscience is a radical extension forward in time of the functioning of State authority. The materials of this attempt to define the contours of the future are necessarily fashioned out of past and present

---

objectively measuring truth and error in sociology is not assumed, the enterprise of the sociology of knowledge is reduced to a naive philosophical relativism. Instead of focusing on the relation of forms of knowledge to the social-substructure, we become involved in an endless controversy as to where the man of knowledge ought to be placed in the earthly constellation. To be sure, it sometimes appears that for Mann-heim the progress of science must be held up pending a settlement of the intelli-gentsia's social position. Mannheim's enormous contributions to the sociology of knowledge notwithstanding, his focusing attention on subsidiary (and at times non-existent) issues, has created a skeptical attitude on the part of scholars who cannot dissociate the discipline from the man.

political relations. Every modern society exhibits coercive, tolerational and libertarian patterns. Societies differ and are distinguished by the quantity of coercion, or the quantity of social permissiveness, or the quantity of liberties, present.

What utopian thought does is universalize one of these features, making it central in any projected reconstruction of society. The utopian mentality further entails an extension in the wish fulfillment phase of consciousness, an idealization of present-day social and economic relations. As a general characteristic, utopia concentrates upon the imaginary contents of the future social order rather than upon the means required to arrive there. The power of utopian thought is the political activity it can generate for the alteration and radicalization of society irrespective of the actual conditions of life. And in its power is also its danger. For utopian thought severs the relation of means and ends, desirable social changes and available instruments for making such changes. The mythic qualities of utopianism can be held uniformly desirable only if we assume that (a) social change is always to be desired, and (b) science can offer no guide to large-scale political decision making. And indeed, the fame of men like Sorel, Mosca and Pareto rests precisely on their willingness to make these two assumptions (Horowitz, 1961: ch. 5).

Let us now turn to a consideration of the three variants in the utopian constellation: coercive utopia, permissive utopia, and libertarian utopia.

The coercive utopia holds central the value of legal order. It is a structuring of future society in such a way that charismatic authority becomes the dominant mode of community organization (Cf. Weber, 1947.) Such a utopia rests consciously upon the idea that power is central to political order, and that order is the key to human perfection. Platonist or Caesarist, intellectual or military, the projection of coercion as morally supreme is a vision in which power values are assigned in an ascending scale leading from the mass groups lacking any power to the elite corps in possession of total power. This elite may be a "circulating" one as in Pareto, a circulation made necessary by internal leadership pressures and external mass pressures, but it never disturbs the gentle balance of terror without disturbing the utopia as such. Securing hierarchical secular order becomes the chief aim of the perfect commonwealth. And it can do so only if all parties to the utopian agreement accept the inviolability of the ruling elite and its bureaucratic apparatus.

The magnetism of the coercive utopia is readily apparent. The absolute supremacy of legal codes ensures a well regulated society in which institutional and individual friction is held to a minimum.

Simmel (1908) offered an interesting commentary on why coercive utopias have attracted so large a following throughout history, irrespective of specific political interests. "How much more easily discords between parties are removed if the parties stand under the same higher power than if each of them is entirely independent. How many conflicts which were the ruin of both Greek and Italian city-States would not have had this destructive consequence if a central power, if some ultimate tribunal, had ruled over them in common! Where there is no such power, the conflict among the elements has the fatal tendency to be fought out only in face to face battle between the power quanta." It is precisely this ideal of the higher tribunal, the delegation of authority and the investment of coercive power in the hands of an elite, that characterized the utopian elements in such traditional philosophers as Plato and Hobbes, and no less the more sophisticated theorizing of Santayana and Russell now. (Cf. Horowitz, 1957.) The coercive utopia commands wide respect precisely for its acknowledgement of the central role of the political-legal machinery in the maintenance of order.

Since for this type of utopia the foundation of the ideal State is social harmony, the means of harnessing conflicts of interest becomes the major question for the truth seeker. Here the role of the charismatic personality is introduced to augment legal coercion. In the framework of the future commonwealth, economic rivalry, community friction, psychological anxiety, are abolished by edict. The dynamic leader, or the tribunal, what Mosca called the "elite of elites," resolves problems of social adjustment and also is sole arbiter of organizing political activity. *Pax Romana* has justifiably come to be known as the generalized expression of that utopian vision which guarantees mass "subjec-

tive" freedom by restricting "objective" freedom to a small core
of decision makers in possession of truth.

The absolute nature of the coercive utopia resides in its consideration of power as the central variable in human affairs. The
difficulty in this utopist *Realpolitik* is that it ignores the fact that
distinctions between those in possession of coercive power and
those coerced, myth-makers and myth-followers, propel men in
the search for ultimate socio-political solutions to begin with.
To employ elitism as the utopian cornerstone is but to replace
present-day imperfect systems of authority with a perfect ideal
authoritarianism. The benefits of this are dubious.

If social order is the basic value attracting people to coercive
forms of utopianism, then with equal assurance it can be said
that personal happiness is the magnet conditioning a faith in
permissive forms of utopianism. The permissive utopia extends
the notion of rights to embrace an ethical concept of the reason-
ableness of men. The materials of this utopia have roots in the
laisser-faire notion of a free functioning man in a free functioning
market economy. It further admits of alternative courses of behaviour in all human enterprise, the best being selected through
the auto-regulation of the rational individual. Permissive utopias
invert the relation of legality and individuality expressed by
coercive doctrines, offering a doctrine of law as a response to
the needs of mass man. Authority is said to come into play only
to mediate the claims of conflicting ego motivations. The permissive utopia corresponds in origins and in theory to the Enlightenment search for the happy man. Education, humanism and
rationalism form the three pillars of the perfect, non-coercive
utopia.

However, this form of utopian mentality disguises rather than
does away with law. The very establishment of a system of
absolute justice tends to re-stratify the social interests of men.
For who is to judge the judges? The permissive utopia must
erect conditions for ethical conduct and rational judgment which
are as binding as the stipulations of coercive utopianism. In
eliminating elitism as an ultimate value, the permissive utopia
subordinates a pre-vision of absolute social order to one of absolute personal happiness. The process of legal mediation between

power groups, rather than the reduction of power to a single unit, becomes the anchor and guarantor of harmony. The moral purposes of the two utopian constellations are clearly different. But whether there is any functional difference between them would depend on the actual relationship between law and human welfare established.

The acute difficulty in the permissive utopia is that it cannot, even in theory, achieve non-coercive standards of regulating behavior. The enforcement of equality simply re-creates legal supremacy, coercion, at a more abstract level. The regulative mechanisms advocated by Maritain (1951) for example, which would establish a world council functioning in terms of ethical and political wisdom, and where decisions would be rendered by "authorities in moral and juridical sciences," only assumes that a non-interest structured elite can be fashioned. It is not what it sets out to be: a system of human relations free of elites. This legal fiction would introduce the idea of a morally responsive and responsible system of coercion, but nonetheless leaves unscathed the human instruments of coercion. And if the purpose of the permissive utopia is to replace coercion with reason, law with man, this sort of benevolent elitism offered as insurance that men are equally entitled to happiness turns a contradictory circle.

Consider the position of Durkheim (1893), which comes close to the ideal commonwealth as seen in permissive utopian terms.

> Men have long dreamt of finally realizing in fact the ideal of human fraternity. People pray for a state where war will no longer be the law of international relations, where relations between societies will be pacifically regulated, as those between individuals already are, where all men will collaborate in the same work, and live the same life. . . . Just as private conflicts can be regulated only by the action of the society in which the individuals live, so intersocial conflicts can be regulated only by a society which comprises in its scope all others. The only power which can serve to moderate individual egotism is the power of the group; the only power which can serve to moderate the egotism of groups, is that of some other group which embraces them.

The ideas of Durkheim on the permissive, non-coercive utopia is fraught with the problem of nothing other than coercion itself.

Durkheim understood that if power is required for the pacific regulation of people, and if this regulative power must in turn be controlled by a yet more inclusive power, where precisely does the possibility of the perfect commonwealth of permissiveness reside?

What invariably takes place is the reduction of permissive utopia into either a form of social prophetism or a doctrine of abstract rights and rules known to all rational men. But either a supernaturalist ethic or the deification of abstract symbols of law, leads to the deterioration of the contents of permissive utopianism. The solution is once more thrown back on the structure and distribution of power, especially political and economic power. The seeds of permissive utopianism paradoxically spreads the disease of coercion by suppressing the question of the control of power and spiritualizing the question of the uses of power. The mediation of the claims of liberty and coercion only succeeds in generating the very social element it seeks to resolve—conflict between men and nations.

The coercive and permissive utopias were both products of past revolutions: the Protestant Reformation and the Bourgeois Revolution respectively. The third form of utopia we are to consider is more recent in time, and has its political sources in the dissolution of and disillusion with the previous two utopian systems. Libertarian utopias are distinguished from permissive varieties by the belief that coercion itself is the chief characteristic of all hitherto existing societies, and must thus be the starting point in any future perfect commonwealth. This differs from the coercive utopias by the insistence on the instrumental value rather than the ethical value of the use of force. The libertarian utopia is also distinguished from the other two by a usually heated denial that its notion of the future organization of man is utopistic. However, these denials are simply verbal bows in the direction of social science.

The point of departure for the libertarian utopia is the claim that in a society of material abundance the need for political coercion to direct public activities vanishes along with human want and misery. Abundance produces rationality, which in turn yields a higher psychology of self-regulation. Such auto-regulation is not a direct product of education, as it is for the permissive utopists, but an indirect consequence of economic security and plentitude. Lenin (1922) could thus write at the end of a polemic against utopianism, against any idea of an easy conquest of abundance and harmony, a commentary which clearly indicates his own faith in the libertarian utopia; a society without a State, beyond democracy, and thus without legal restraints.

> From the moment when all members of society, or even only the overwhelming majority, have learned how to govern the State *themselves*, have taken this business into their own hands, have established control over the insignificant minority of capitalists, over the gentlemen with capitalist leanings, and the workers thoroughly demoralized by capitalism—from this moment the need for any government begins to disappear. The more complete the democracy, the nearer the moment when it begins to be unnecessary. The more democratic the "State" consisting of armed workers, which is "no longer a State in the proper sense of the word," the more rapidly does every State begin to wither away.

It is clear from this type of statement that libertarian utopia, despite its hostility to rationalistic or pacific formulations of the utopian vision, is no less committed to a like speculation and projection of the ultimate good society. It is hardly scientific to declare that since productivity and psychology would reach new levels, that this guarantees that the future society will develop in such a way that the uses of coercion would be made superfluous. Lenin himself employs a Platonic maneuver to escape the implications of the libertarian utopia. He distinguishes between State power and the power of the armed guardians of the nation. This, however, simply indicates a change in the emanation of power and in the distribution of elites. It offers nothing about the elimination of coercion and elitism in general.

The complex social formations which accompany scientific and technological change create unforeseeable problems in the total spectrum of civilization. The existing levels of human interaction tend to reduce long-range predictions to either platitudes or tautologies. With the absence of sufficient information as to the contours of society even in a relatively short period of a century hence, and the corresponding difficulties of blocking out statistical data to yield such information, the insistence that coercion will become a political superfluity is empirically undecidable. This does not mean that the reduction or elimination of the coercive features of a society is a worthless objective. It does mean that the moral worth of an object is no guarantee of its taking place in the realm of material culture.

What underlies the libertarian utopia is faith in a strict correlation of economic equality and political democracy. Whether one raises objections to such a mechanical correlation offered by classical political philosophy, or by direct appeals to the actual functioning of present-day socio-economic systems as different as American capitalism and Russian communism, it is difficult to see how the pure libertarian commonwealth can escape from the inherent characteristics of the utopian vision as a whole.

The paradox of libertarian utopias is that they generally hold coercion itself to be the main instrument of their elimination. The machinery of the State is galvanized into action to secure the libertarian vision. The libertarian complex cleaves in two: either it becomes a faith in the free conscience, or it places the arrival of the good commonwealth in an indefinite future closed to any exact predictions. This cleavage is philosophically significant, since it demarcates the line between liberalism and socialism. But since ultimate goals and values are essentially similiar for both strands of the utopian vision, analytically they share the same paradoxes.

Social order, the ideal of the coercive utopists, the *bête noire* of permissive utopists, becomes the chief instrument for realizing the libertarian utopia. In none of the three perspectives does the functioning elite evaporate. What remains is the ancient prophetic attempt to whip society into shape for the eternal march into the future. Utopian vision is not, on this account, a series of errors. It carries in all its forms the germs of serious and specific social protest. In so doing it often anticipates the direction of human strivings. At the same time it never ceases to function as social metaphysics. The scientific determination of social change is never enough for the true utopian: partial solutions, plural options, and probable changes do not satiate the utopian palate. The fashioning of future commonwealths out

of precarious proximate values like coercion, toleration and freedom, is the reply of utopian consciousness to the oppressiveness
of the dominant ideology, and no less to the intrinsic restrictions
of the social sciences. Beyond physics is metaphysics, and beyond
social science is utopianism.

But on these grounds to deny cognitive value to utopian constellations, to endow them with visionary content alone, is to miss
the point as to how popular response to utopian appeals can
occur. An appreciation of the limits and shortcomings of utopian
theory can be made without denying that in its kernel is a critique
of existing social iniquities. New and even improved social conditions do not eliminate problems, but only transform the nature
of such problems. The velocity of change in society makes the
utopia of today the reality of tomorrow, and sometimes, the night-
mare of the day after tomorrow. (Cf. Riesman, 1950: ch. 16.)

Like ideology, utopia falls between truth and error, and at no
point is either one or the other. The double conscience of utopianism moves in contrasting directions: when left in the realm
of futuristic images, it degenerates into a form of mysticism and
phantasy that is never aware of real, if partial, human advances;
but the utopian vision can also act as a stimulant to social activity
by prodding social science beyond itself into newer areas of
exploration.

Chapter IX

Laws and Levels in the Sociology of Knowledge

RIESMAN recently noted that sociology came into being as a revolt against the genteel tradition of attempts to set up some orders of data as hierarchically superior to others (1959: 280). While it is true as far as data selection is concerned, the same cannot be said for sociological methodologies. Statisticians disparage the worth of functional analysis. Functionalists claim a value neutrality absent in historical sociology, which in turn considers the results of the structural-functional school as correct but trivial. Sociological knowledge itself has become suspect as a result of this ideological battle between empiricists and historicists. While I do not propose within the confines of this essay to construct a sociology of sociology, I would like to show that this methodological battle rests on the false assumption that a scientific explanation can be arrived at by only one type of method. (Cf. Braithwaite, 1953:ch.XI.)

The sociology of knowledge, by employing a wide variety of sociological systems, has shown that alternative explanations of the same phenomenon are possible, and indeed can facilitate a complete understanding of any given problem. It is not the purpose of the sociology of knowledge to multiply explanations, but rather to fit its methods and theories to the particular problem under consideration. This requires several kinds of systems. Suppose our task is that of an admissions officer to determine whether a given school is best for a particular individual student. He will have to take into account and weigh such intellective factors as scores on college entrance examinations, grades received at the secondary school, strongest areas of competence and career interests. The admissions officer must also weigh less tangible data, letters of recommendation, the home environment of the candidate, and perhaps other factors such as sex, age, military service, etc. The final decision is clearly a composite of the operative factors. There is no logical reason for the sociology of knowledge to do less. This is not to say that uniformly good results must follow, any more so than a weighing of all factors in selecting a student for a given college is proof of that student's capacity. But the alternative is the collapse of a theory of measurement altogether.

The social roots of knowledge are rarely discoverable by utilizing a single system of scientific explanation. Even if we agree to a system of primary and secondary factors of analysis, it does not change the need to make the widest use of differing laws and levels of social theory. (Cf. Zilsel, 1941.) This does not involve the reduction of every problem in knowledge to statistical correlates. The structuring of problems implies a system of operations which will symbolize and abstract the phenomena under investigation with a minimum of distortion. This is done by first grouping facts into hypothesis and law statements, and then by describing the initial and limiting conditions of an experimental situation. (Cf. Hempel, 1942.) The object of any social science is the acquisition of truths about how men function. If this object can be gained by one avenue, one method, well and good. If this objective requires a plurality of approaches, several analytical devices, well and good. But to make such truths the property of methodology is to convert instruments for study into the objects of study. Such an approach has more in common with solipsism than science.

For our purposes, we can subdivide the instruments employed by the sociology of knowledge (in common with sociology in general) into six types, often used in conjunction with one another, and sometimes used separately. They are (1) mathematical and statistical analysis, (2) functionalist theory, (3) paradigms and linguistic typologies, (4) field theories, (5) ideal typologies, (6) historical models. What is inextricably involved in the sound use of any of these kinds of approaches is a distortion-free description of a slice of reality. The very ability to distinguish bias elements from truth elements indicates that a core of useful results are possible, whatever the social position of the investigator. The further refinement of a concept of levels should increase the practical value of any of these six instruments of analysis.

The development of a concept of levels within a unified language of the social sciences, can strengthen the synthetic goals of the sociologist of knowledge in particular. The sound use of ordinary or symbolic language systems can clarify the relationship between social field theories, generic types, causal determinations, historical tendencies and laws, and even the ethical description of these various models. What a given society does with a particular complex of ideas, *vis a vis* other societies or individuals, is a relative matter. Similarly, questions in the obsolescence of social theories, the political uses of the same ideas by different interest groups, may require a multiple form of explanation. The logical structuring of these forms of explanation is insurance that these explanations remain open to further investigation, i.e., to make sure that such insights do not assume a private or arbitrary character. Novikoff summed this up by noting that "each level of organization possesses unique properties of structure and behavior which, though dependent on the properties of the constituent elements, appear only when these elements are combined in the new system. The laws describing the unique properties of each level are qualitatively distinct, and their discovery requires methods of research and analysis appropriate to the particular level." (Cf. Herrick, 1949:226.)

The chief point is that the instruments used in scientific study must be determined by the level of phenomena under analysis. (Cf. Edel, 1949, 1959a.) To brood over the "existential absurdities" of human desires in contrast to human realizations, or to declare a problem "meaningless" if it cannot be explained by any single methodological tool, is to reduce social science to a series of false alternatives, the upshot of which would be the decimation of science and not the liberation of men from ignorance. For this reason, I shall treat the six methods of analysis used in the sociology of knowledge as co-existent rather than as mutually exclusive. What requires steady emphasis is that the object of knowledge can be approached through many avenues. Time enough exists *after* the object has been gained to develop and create simpler operational procedures.

The increased attention of sociology to the possibilities of attacking problems, which in past ages were thought insoluble by experimental means, indicates a mature attitude to problems of method and content. This has been done by a process of formalization, i.e., the conversion of problems from an object-language into a logical meta-language. This would seem to be the burden of Lazarsfeld's comment (1954) on mathematical thinking in contemporary sociology.

> The man who carries out experiments or makes concrete observations on a phenomenon of social interaction finds himself confronted with so many factors that he can no longer cope with them adequately in an intuitive and discursive way. But the great system builders also, who do not concern themselves with these innumerable details, now work in a different intellectual climate. A hundred years ago the task seemed to make sweeping guesses as to the future development of society. Fifty years ago the interest focused in basic concepts which would properly classify the crucial social phenomena. Today the trend is toward singling out the basic variables from which all specific concepts and interrelationships can be derived. Even those who do not believe in an early use of mathematics try to utilize some rudiments of formalization, in order to clarify their underlying assumptions, and to derive specific findings from more general models.

Lazarsfeld and others, like Festinger and Katz (1953), may be exaggerating the point when they say that the tasks no less than the methods of sociological research have shifted. There is, however, a clear sense in which new methods have opened up new possibilities of the social study of knowledge. Such enterprises as the standardization of data processing, the objectification of sample surveys and techniques, the use of public records and documents, these are but some of the ways the shift from intuition to analysis has expressed itself in sociology. (Cf. Likert and Lippitt, 1953: ch. 13.)

As Neurath indicated (1932; 1944:ch.7), even those thoroughly convinced of the superiority of analytic sociology are divided on the question of just how far a mathematical scheme can be extended without making a fetish out of the ideal of complete precision. A clear gap exists between a quantification technique for measuring the intensities or probabilities of recurrent events, and problems which require the correlation of nonrecurrent topological events. Bunge (1959) has shown that different measurements are required for demonstrating intensities and the topological order of qualities. This being the case, a complete sociological explanation, even of such apparently statistical questions as income distribution and redistribution, requires the use of non-quantitative information. For the problems of income distribution one would have to know the occupational patterns of a particular group in material production. Similarly, to study the cultural patterns of the same group, we would have to have, in addition to intelligence test reports, a knowledge of older inherited culture patterns affecting results of the tests. But the question of the extent to which a given problem can be quantified is one of practical limits, and does not *apriori* signify the impossibility of an increased use of mathematical models in social research. (Cf. Greenberg, 1959:ch.14, Zetterberg, 1954:533-39.)

Problems in the sources of science, education and religious belief have thus far received limited attention along the lines of applied mathematics. But the efforts made indicate wider possibilities for axiomatic systems to cover such phenomena. Efforts have been made to systematize the relationship between behavior and belief by the use of objective standardized questionnaires and field theory techniques. (Cf. Rosenberg, 1955.) The work of Cantril and his associates (1940) along these lines is particularly worth mentioning. His development of an auditing system for checking the extent and quality of belief in a fictitious "invasion from Mars" indicates the potential of mathematical and statistical information for the sociology of knowledge. Cantril's statistical research proved to be a test case for checking mass credulity to fiction presented in a "realistic" manner and in a climate of public opinion receptive to cataclysmic undertakings. His study reveals the number of individuals ready and willing to check their information, the extent of mass faith in media of communications, the degree to which personal wish-fulfillment attitudes condition responses to problems of a troubled world, and more generally, the degree of anxiety required to transform personal fear into vicarious or destructive patterns of behavior. The recent studies of Adorno (1950) and Lazarsfeld and Katz (1955), employing more refined techniques of applied mathematics, have extended Cantril's work into such diverse areas as the causes of anti-semitism, and the role of personal influence in conditioning attitudes on everything from politics to pills. Employed in this way, and admitting the hypothetical nature of the results, applied mathematics forms a basis for higher level analysis (i.e., beyond the sociology of small groups) in the sociology of knowledge and in social psychology.

Quantification of social science problems along such lines is, however, a somewhat mixed blessing. While useful for many levels of analysis, the endless multiplication of mathematical models in sociology lacking in meaning or use, can serve biased professional interests over and above the needs of the behavioral sciences. Gillin's (1954) sociological statement on this tendency to multiply theories at the expense of reality cannot be dismissed easily, particularly by those who see in mathematics the ultimate answers to present problems in the behavioral sciences.

> Since a social scientist can seldom by the practice of his profession win "distinction" measured in monetary terms, it is not surprising that other ways are sought by some. Often the desired goal seems to be defined as "being different from others," that is, being "distinct" rather than "distinguished" in other senses. So far as work on consolidated theory of human behavior is concerned, this tendency on occasion has had the effect of cluttering the field with a variety of ostensibly theoretical statements that are purposely (if unconsciously) irreconcilable. The authors of such theories, together with their respective students and friends, can make careers of "defending their positions" and "counter-attacking the opposition," without ever adding appreciably to our shared scientific knowledge.

Of course, there is no doubt that the more serious-minded behavioral scientists have struggled to avoid this. But there can also be no doubt that the championing of applied mathematics as the sole system for realizing sociological results has resulted in that endless multiplication of theories Gillin talks of, and no less in the creation of an artificially pure model of social research that ends up by being more utopian than the intuitively derived sociologies of the last century. (Cf. Dahrendorf, 1958; Mills, 1959.)

However great the impact of mathematical thinking on the social sciences, the main theoretical prop of modern sociology remains the functionalism of the school of Merton and Parsons. Since the most complete statement on functionalism is contained in the paradigm of Merton's famous study, "Manifest and Latent Functions" (1957:19-84), and since Nagel presents the functionalist canons of Merton once again in his own study, "A Formalization of Functionalism" (1957:247-83), there is no need to present them yet another time. What I should like to do, therefore, is briefly formalize the expository portions of Merton's essay, so that the reader can have before him a complete itemization of the theoretical basis of functional analysis.

Merton's theoretical formulation of functionalism can be summed up under the following six points: (a) Persisting cultural and social forms have a net balance of functional consequences, either for society as a whole or any of its sub-groups. (b) Just as the same situational matrix may have multiple functions, so too, the same function may be diversely fulfilled by alternative matrices. (c) The concept of function involves the permissibility of alternatives and the retention of alternatives. One need not make the assumption that any given functional matrix is indispensable for the continuation and maintenance of a society. (d) A functional approach is neither intrinsically conservative nor radical in its political and ideological moorings. It is only at the evaluational level that functional analysis can be employed for varied political goals. (e) The logical sequence of functional analysis reveals four stages: the need of a function for the survival and maintenance of a social organism; an account through which these societal requirements are met; lacking the function held necessary for survival, one must seek compensatory mechanisms; and last, an account of the structure for which and through which a function exists and is fulfilled. (f) In sum, functional analysis is the practice of interpreting information by establishing their consequences in terms of higher order matrices in which a function is implanted and implicated.

Not the least merit in Merton's analysis is that he tells us what a function is not from a sociological point of view. On three counts, there can be no ambiguity. That is, sociology does not employ function to signify: a public gathering (popular usage), an occupation (economic usage), or to denote office-holding (political sense). As for the next two senses in which sociology apparently does not use the word function, there is quite a good deal of ambiguity. Merton indicates that the term function is not used as a variable considered in relation to one or more variables (mathematical usage), or as a vital or organic process considered in relation to the constitution or evolution of an organism (biological usage). However, despite this disavowal, there does indeed seem to be a reliance on Merton's part, and the functional-structural school generally, of evidence accumulated by the biological and physiological uses of the term function.

It is just this biological point of reference in functionalism that seems to have inspired Nagel's statement and criticism. The points made by Nagel raise some genuine issues, which everyone concerned with the practice of sociology or social theory must consider if a durable statement on laws and levels in sociology is to be reached. The eight criticisms made by Nagel would indicate that functionalism, far from exhausting the problem of laws and levels in social research, is best considered as one type of possible instrument for delving into such issues.

The position of Nagel can be summarized in the following way: (a) Functional statements either in biology or sociology can be so constructed as to deliberately avoid functional or purposive languages. Thus functional statements are forms through which problems can be appraised, giving selective emphasis rather than actual causal descriptions of problems themselves. (b) The term function can be employed in so many ways that even screening out five possibilities, as Merton does, goes but a short distance towards a refined notion of social function. (c) Functional interpretation of events, or even functional language, is by no means uniform in the sciences. For while biology employs this language often enough, functional concepts but rarely find their way into modern physics. (d) By a series of logical notations, we are able to disprove the thesis that functions establish necessary correlations. That is, in any given system "S" the trait "G" may operate in large measure as an independent variable, rather than as a functionally interdependent variable. The values of a system are thus not automatically derivable from the traits of that system. Functional dependence is therefore a matter to be settled empirically and not logically. (e) The distinctions drawn between types of functions, latent and manifest, are vacuous, since all functions are in some sense a combination of both. (f) The construction of a typology of functional systems which would offer a hierarchy among them requires material assumptions that fall quite outside the scope or capacity of functional analysis. (g) This introduces a more general critique of functionalism, that no mention is made of the environment or other material relations in which any real function is embedded. Thus, functionalism admits of no laws, only statements of co-ordinates which are assumed to control social change. (h) Nagel's concluding point is that problems are reserved for functional analysis that are properly within the general province of social science. Such issues as the role of ideological distortion of scientific premises, or the problem of validating assumptions and imputations, which Merton raises in connection with his discussion of functionalism, are no less treated by non-functional levels of sociology.

Nagel's critique presented, it should be added that his aim is not to eliminate functional analysis in sociological work. Quite the reverse, he indicates that the central task, the formalization of functionalism, is not only desirable but possible. And if great profit could be derived by Merton, Parsons, and their associates, by using as a model the functionalist concepts employed in the biological sciences, even greater possibilities can be expected once the edge of the mathematical razor is applied. If I understand Nagel rightly, this he would do by more precise accounting on the part of the functionalists about the level at which they are operating; the level of co-ordinates framed; clearing up the ambiguities involved in using analogies derived from biology and mathematics without discriminating between empirical and log-cal functions; distinguishing the system in which functions are made from other field systems; and finally by so focusing on the traits of a system being studied that such things as ideologies and value-judgments are either eliminated from the results or accounted for in the process of social analysis.

Nagel has largely confined his criticisms to the paradigm of functionalism, restricting his remarks to the logical, rather than the epistemological status of functionalism. The result was to preserve functional analysis from an unconscious commitment to teleology. We can surmise that for Nagel, functionalism does not replace so much as augment a naturalistic philosophy. On the other hand, the distinct impression is left by Merton that functionalism can properly be viewed as more than methodology, and perhaps as something more than the logic of the social sciences. We are thus offered the rare (but nonetheless welcome) paradox of the philosopher claiming less for functionalism than the empirical sociologist. Nonetheless, functionalism is a fundamental break with the historicist tradition in that it rules out metaphysical efforts to explain social events. It seems to me that the main work of functional analysis is not just to iron out its technical dilemmas, but to offer more in the way of theoretical foundations.

Merton may be correct in denying that functionalism has intrinsic ideological components, but this seems to me to be circumventing the main issue. What is at stake is the valuational basis, rather than the ideological superstructure. It is the conscious decision in favor of functionalism that needs more adequate justification, not the nature of unconscious mechanisms of belief. What are the implicit values involved in judging social structures on the basis of their ability to work and survive? For if one can judge a social system in terms of its survival or adaptive capacities, this does not exclude the possibility of using alternative norms, such as the rate of economic growth, the population curve, or even more ephemeral measurements like the degree of militarization in a society. While it might be said that a functional approach is necessary to avoid ideological pitfalls, this does not necessarily exclude the need for a deeper study of the value systems implicit in functional systems. Even granting the claim of Merton that functionalism is ideology-free, it remains an urgent task to free functionalism from the pragmatic valve of workability, by making more explicit the character of its presently all too malleable assumptions.

Another objection can be launched against Merton's claim of having achieved, through functionalism, a level of analysis that defies descriptions such as radical or conservative. This may be true at the first level of functional analysis, at the logical level, but at the level of value predicates this clearly cannot be maintained. Merton cites Alexis Carrel and Albert Einstein as men who, with quite different intellectual attitudes, share a common functionalist approach. Let us pursue the matter, and take the notion of the improvement of the human species, a subject dear to Carrel and Einstein alike. Can it be seriously entertained that Carrel, advocating everything from the hygienic purification of the race to racial genocide, shared in the same value predicates as Einstein, the advocate of humanism, socialism and the force of education? Functionalism operates by ignoring the degree to which value predicates have profound repercussions at the functional layer of analysis.

The extent to which goals implicitly or explicitly frame functions is a matter for empirical determination, and is itself not necessarily committed to a functional account. The functional-structural school of sociology is running the steady risk of evaluating everything other than itself. As of now, functional analysis has mastered the formal and comparative levels of society. It has not done much in the way of causal explanation. One danger in functionalism is its oft-repeated assumption that an assignment of strict correlations in the form of co-ordinates precludes the need for an assignment of causal priorities. However, if functionalism may be viewed as one index of possibilities, in a given contextual situation, then the material or causal level of scientific explanation can still be examined, by methods geared to solve causal issues, i.e., by measurements in terms of time as well as space, historically as well as analytically.

The lasting worth of functional analysis in the behavioral sciences is to redirect our energies from the most abstract speculative problems to the most concrete social concerns. It has taught us the advisability of a sociology that starts with the data supplied from social relations, rather than consider society as something to be explained from outside, from metaphysical or theological predispositions. Functionalism has shown, haltingly to be sure, that if we start with facts we may realize meaningful theoretical constructions, but that if we start with theoretical constructs drawn from ideological needs, it becomes difficult, if not impossible, to get to the facts.

One of the chief by-products of functional analysis in sociology has been the develepoment of paradigms as a basis for comparing studies which appear in the same area. The paradigm, which began as a formal schematization of a set of hypotheses or theories pertaining to a given field of investigation, has now grown into a methodological device for the reduction of problems to a logically consistent model. Its uses have been particularly evident in the growth of an empirical sociology of knowledge. And again, it has been the work of Merton (1945) that has given substance to the use of paradigms in the social studies.

The purposes of the paradigm are to offer a classificatory system that can account for all the aspects of a given frame of reference, an inventory of extant findings, an indication of the consistency of results achieved and conceptual apparatus used, and also to assess the nature and the quality of the evidence brought into play. The paradigm is thus not so much a method of investigation as a formal mode of investigating the investigators. The five factors said to constitute the skelton of any study in the sociology of knowledge offered by Merton is indicative of the nature and scope of the paradigmal form. "Where *is the existential basis of mental productions located?* . . . What *mental productions are being sociologically analyzed?* . . . How *are mental productions related to the existential basis?* . . . Why? *Manifest and latent functions imputed to these existentially conditioned mental productions.* . . . When *do the imputed relations of the existential base and knowledge obtain?*"

A significant use of the paradigm has been the blocking out of unsystematic work into a systematic form. This enables the investigator to get at the logical core of a position, if indeed the core is found to be logical. When used with restraint and care so as not to omit the major features of any given survey, the results can be illuminating. The tabulations by Merton of Znaniecki's types of social roles of men of knowledge (1941); the paradigm of leadership qualities presented by Seeman and Morris (1950); and the more recent paradigm by Wolff of Merton's comparison between the sociology of knowledge and mass communications analysis (1959), are examples of how the paradigm form contributes to a deeper understanding of the formal structure of studies in sociology.

Nonetheless, I do not believe that the paradigm can ever be more than a tabulation, or a compilation of various empirical studies. By itself, the paradigm can achieve no results, nor even serve as a theoretical guide in experimental work. One of the difficulties is that those who use the paradigm are not always willing to consider it as an extension of the formal elements in a social science methodology. Instead, it is often employed as a substitute for concrete analysis itself. This appears particularly the case in Parsons' efforts to work out a general theory of the social structure on the basis of types of human action. Gouldner's (1959) critique of this new formalism deserves to be cited at some length, not only as a characterization of shortcomings in the work of Parsons, but as an account of how a formal device such as the paradigm can be made to substitute for empirical research.

Parson's theory of the social system leads research attention away from *systematic* efforts to develop and validate generalized propositions concerning the manner in which ecological and other properties of the physical environment of groups structure patterns of social organization. In exiling these from the social system, Parsons at best derives a purely formal advantage, namely that of establishing a distinct class of systems which may form the object of an independent social science. But in doing this he fails to make a systematic place for numerous cogent researches which, if lacking in formal elegance in this sense, do illuminate the important ways in which social behavior is structured by ecological forces. To constitute the social system thusly may well accomplish the objective of establishing a charter for an inde-

pendent social science. But it may be a Pyrrhic victory bought at
the cost of a scientific ritualism, where logical elegance is sub-
stituted for empirical potency.

The burden of Gouldner's remarks are clear: the symmetry of a
formal system is no adequate substitute for empirical researches,
no matter how asymmetrical they turn out. Indeed, if too much
faith is placed on formal elegance of a method, as seems to be
the case with the current usage of the paradigm, sociological
theory runs the risk of substituting esthetic criteria for empirical
criteria. While it may often be the case that the inability to
place a study in paradigm form is evidence that such a study is
illogical or vaporous, such an inability may also be due to the
complexities of the issues under consideration. The "value-free"
paradigm, like the value-free functional variable, suffers from an
overdose of formalism that tends to disguise rather than eliminate
the role of ethical norms in the structuring of social theories.

The levels and models in social theory thus far considered have
a consciously limited range of applicability. Mathematical sociology, statistical sociology, functional analysis, and the paradigm
form of stating problems, are geared to solving short-range problems by the use of available empirical data rigorously applied.
As such, these levels in social theory are more concerned with
stated opinions than with unconscious use and distortions of systems of knowledge; isolated aggregates of information rather
than systematic doctrinal knowledge. (Cf. Merton, 1957:439-55.)
These approaches have sometimes been called the essential characteristic of American social theory, in contrast to the European
tradition of sociology (particularly *Wissenssoziologie*) of intu-
itive-philosophical approaches, where reliability of data is of
little consequence.

While it is clear that there are manifest differences between
American and European variants of social theory, having their
sources in different intellectual and practical climates, there are
too many exceptions on either side of the ocean to establish even
a phase rule concerning differences. What I think is more to
the point is that those who operate on the aforementioned strict
empirical levels, can hardly do more than select and sample

public opinion without moving beyond the confines of the available data. While those interested in the formation of higher-order explanation, that is a more synthetic hypothetical system, cannot consider limitations of data as necessary limitations on theory construction. This is a situation to be found in the natural and biological sciences as well. Why this distinction between levels of theory has created so many difficulties in sociology has, I should say, more to do with the marketing orientation of social research in America than with any intrinsic theoretical obstacles.

Turning now to the work of Kurt Lewin, we find a representative effort to strike a balance between strict regard for evidence and an attempt to create a theoretical edifice that can be used for high-order generalization and long-range prediction. His work in social psychology illustrates the growing awareness that it is no longer possible to expect the behavioural sciences to conform to physicalist models following definite stages from definition, assumption, to conclusion. Lewin's own work is to show the *determinierende Tendenz,* or the determined tendencies of a particular field of operational relevance. Basic to his "system of tension" is that in every such field, there is an association of human forces polarized around the question of social change. The field is thus a dynamic interplay of those with and without an intrinsic tendency to create a change. The coordination of these two, the examination of opposing and yet inter-related forces, is what Lewin terms the field level of analysis. (Cf. Lewin, 1917:212-47.)

Lewin notes that this approach differs considerably from the character of physical laws, since in physics if one proceeds from a special law or theory to more general and inclusive theories, one does not finally come to a field theory. This is because physical laws are operative at a different and lower level of use and meaning than social laws. Field theory, on the other hand, is more a methodology than a theory in the pure sense. It is a method for analyzing causal relations and of building social science constructs expressed in the form of general statements about the nature and conditions of human change. (Cf. Lewin, 1951:45.) In this attempt to consider behavior as a function of the total social situation, Lewin was compelled to go beyond his early prejudice in favor of the diagrammatic and statistical, into the most "reified" area of the social sciences, psychoanalysis. By this amalgam of objective data and subjective responses to given situations, Lewin opened up possible areas of integration of field theory to a level of scientific conceptualization that would base itself on changes in the cognitive content of human perception and judgment (1948).

The root contribution of Lewin to a sociology of knowledge was to show that before analysis of a given type of knowledge can be effectively made, it is first necessary to translate statements of ideas into corresponding statements of behaviour.

This scientific determination of the relation of bodies of knowledge to fields of behaviour involves a high degree of selectivity. The field under investigation must be large enough to render meaningful predictions of future action, and yet small enough for extracting precise data. Predictions turn into platitudes if one cannot state the conditions for the failure (as well as success) of a forecast.

Parsons' (1951) efforts to work out the knowledge elements in a set of human actions, indicate some of the dangers of Lewin's effort to translate knowledge into behavioural patterns. Parsons divides his elements into the following: (a) cathetic elements, those forces that require evaluation in terms of the gratification or deprivation that an action might bring to the individual; (b) cognitive elements, the purposive estimate of the consequences any act might bring about by the use of objective tests; and (c) temporal elements, the structuring of a situation in terms of anticipations and goals, i.e., things awaited passively in contrast to things derived from purposive behaviour. Worthwhile as this sort of blocking out of the field might prove to be, it would have to be recast. For since Lewin and Parsons do not explain what an action is not, there seems no way of meaningfully describing what an action situation is. Any empirical studies using field techniques must not only be able to translate bodies of knowledge into fields of behaviour, but must also determine the limits of such symbolic translations. And in order to do this, we must still state the differences between knowledge and action, not just arbitrarily claim that they are really the same. The propensity of field theory analysis to confuse and confound the empirical and the formal, the descriptive and the logical, would indicate that a higher level of generalization, with a more inclusive range of admissible criteria, is needed to determine the cycle of human knowledge and social behaviour.

One such notable attempt at greater inclusiveness in measuring the worth of social theory is Max Weber's concept of ideal types. As Martindale notes, "for Weber the ideal type contains both conceptual and observational materials, both being required for the type. Such conceptual and observational materials are not put together arbitrarily. The relationships expressed in a type are such as 'our imagination accepts as plausibly motivated and hence as objectively possible and which appear as *adequate* from the nomological standpoint.' Objective possibility and adequate causation are the criteria for forming conceptual and observational materials into a type" (1959:69).

The aim of Weber's ideal typology, whether used analytically or historically, is to explicate the unique character of cultural phenomena, rather than to explain class or average behavior. Critics of Weber's "Kantian idealism" have tended to overlook this limit Weber placed on the ideal-type approach. A hypothesis is tested in terms of measuring actual socio-historical developments by existing typologies, constructions based on a causal conception of past events. Thus, when Marx postulates a general theory of evolution by the number of classes and men emancipated from economic exploitation, this for Weber becomes an ideal-type. Historical materialism becomes a theory of *measuring* the velocity of social change, rather than an actual description of change as such. The validity of Marxian historical materialism, or Comtian positivism, was thus considered as relative to the social problem being treated. While any theoretical construction differs from the actual course of events, that construction which comes closest to describing and predicting the largest number of discrete events is clearly best, scientifically speaking. (Cf. Weber, 1949.)

The ideal type becomes important in: (a) measuring the distance between the theoretically possible and the practically occurrent, (b) connecting up in causal sequence historical events thought to be discrete, (c) revealing divergencies between social change from nation to nation, and smaller or larger units of social existence. What is particularly important for the sociology of knowledge in Weber's formation of an ideal typology is that, even if our analytical guides are something less than purely scientific, even if they are bound by social interests of a class or group, it is nonetheless possible to frame some high-order generalizations having predictive value. The process of abstracting, and even exaggerating certain features in the social system, is no proof that historical knowledge is without use. Indeed, since no theoretical construction is considered by Weber to be a seat of ultimate wisdom, the degree to which such ideal constructs show deviations from actual events, becomes a chief undertaking of the sociologist. In other words, the mere presence of intense social commitments to certain political goals may be an aid as well as a handicap in explaining the present and in predicting the future.

The prime limitation of a system of ideal-types is that, while it measures the relation of theoretical systems to the actual course of events, it holds out little promise for the scientific explanation of history. Weber, under the spell of what Honigsheim (1950) terms "Neo-Kantian Protestantism," drew a particularly sharp distinction between science and history, the special sciences and the cultural sciences. As Honigsheim succinctly sums up Weber's attitude: "History primarily deals with the uniqueness of the particular object observed. Thus, within the sphere of historical observations, general terms such as animal husbandry, nomadism, feudalism, bureaucracy, state, etc. can and must be used; but, in so doing, one must have in mind that such terms actually are nothing but abbreviations. They are used to denote the sum of all these particular historical subjects, which have the same characteristic traits in common. There is no possibility of knowing about the existence or non-existence of an entity in the metaphysical sense corresponding in reality to these terms. Moreover, within the sphere of historical investigations, it is impossible to make statements concerning automatically occurring changes" (1950:11-12). Thus, the ideal typology affords correlations of logical rather than epistemological significance. But the problem of historical knowledge is a problem precisely because there is a sense in which historical statements are cognitively verifiable. Now that the anti-historicist fervor in the social sciences has considerably cooled, it is possible to take a longer look at the value of historical evidence in the formation of sociological rules and laws.

Historical law as a possible level of social existence has been a hotly debated issue since the time of Hegel. Some scholars, like Isaiah Berlin (1954) have disputed all claims for a historical science on either predictive or descriptive grounds. Even those, like Passmore (1958), who would grant history some descriptive value, deny it a scientific status by claiming historical statements to be lacking in either prescriptive or predictive power. The most persuasive critic of historical evidence was Nietschze (1874), who considered his age overrun by a "malignant historical fever," and set down various objections that remain the hard core of present-day objections to the use of historical evidence in the social sciences. Nietzsche sums up his position in the following way:

> An excess of history seems to be an enemy of the life of a time, and dangerous in five ways. Firstly, the contrast of *inner* and *outer* is emphasized and personality weakened. Secondly, the time comes to imagine that it possesses the rarest of virtues, justice, to a higher degree than any other time. Thirdly, the instincts of a nation are thwarted, the maturity of the individual arrested no less than that of the whole. Fourthly, we get the belief in the old age of mankind, the belief, at all times harmful, that we are late survivals, mere epigoni. Lastly, an age reaches a dangerous condition of irony with regard to itself, and the still more dangerous state of cynicism, when a cunning egoistic theory of action is matured that maims and at last destroys the vital strength.

For all of its driving, passionate defense of the moral man against immoral history, the voluntarism of Nietzsche is simply a reproduction of the criticisms made by contemporary existentialists against science in general. The reason history seems to have been so singularly criticized is that the nature of its evidence, being more linked to documents of the past than data of the present, seems too inexact to be of service in predicting future events, or even in causal explanation of past events. And if, in addition to its imprecision, it is, as Nietzsche says, a compendium of human immorality, then it should be ruled out of the behavioural sciences forevermore.

But there are two large-scale "ifs" involved. And as we have seen the degree of exactness of a given science is a quantitative issue that does not automatically qualify or disqualify any body of evidence from the realm of science. Further, there is no evidence to prove the thesis that men are more immoral if they accept historical evidence, then there is any evidence that true morality must fly in the face of history. Thus both the positivist and romanticist objections seem to rest on an exaggerated fear that historical evidence somehow is part of either the unscientific or the immoral.

Historical statements have the same practical status as a medical statement. A diagnosis either in medicine or of a society simply asserts the likely consequences of performing or not performing an activity in accordance with the best available information. The many dialogues in criticism or in defense of history have the same epistemological status as works defending or attacking the belief in social determinism. But history need not be viewed as a matter of logical proofs. The degree of determination is always relative to the available information and on the capacities of the investigator to uncover such historical "secrets." Historical determinism is not an all-or-nothing affair, but a more-or-less condition. This being the status of most empirical statements, the need to bemoan the probabilistic status of historical laws has to be considered as a psychological desire for certainty. An assumption is made by Nietzsche and Sorel that certainty produces a higher quantity of action than if men always weigh probabilities. But this assumption, whether correct or not, has no necessary implications for the actual procedures of historical investigations. The solution for improper diagnosis is more carefully screened diagnosis. Criticism of the worth of historical diagnosis, setting arbitrary limits to the deterministic principle, would involve a return to sophistry and spiritualism. And as Nagel recently summed matters up in an article on history: "to abandon the deterministic principle itself, is to withdraw from the enterprise of science" (Nagel, 1960:317).

It is in this diagnostic sense that historical investigations can be used to assist the sociology of knowledge to determine the sources and distortions in idea systems. History is always the history of some given object, person, community or nation. There is no history apart from changes in the structure of reality. To deny history a place in the behavioural sciences is therefore an affirmation of the unknowability of the processes taking place in the world. The groundless fear that history marks the end of freedom is soundly refuted by the classic historians themselves. As Joynt (1956) says:

> One of the objections to the view that historical laws are objective regularities rather than mental constructs is the erroneous belief that historical determinism is equivalent to fatalism. This would mean that the advocacy of political and social action would be inconsistent with the belief in the objectivity of social laws. For example, it is often argued that Marx was precluded by his own theory of historical determinism from advocating changes in the structure of society on the alleged grounds that his theory presumably predicted the occurrence of these changes independently of such action. The fallacy in any argument of this type against historical determinism (the Marxian form of historical determinism being only one) is that "the system concerning which a historical determinist makes a prediction *ab extra* can easily be one in which he is a causal agent along with others who desire to achieve certain goals and who urge still others to share these ambitions" (Grünbaum, 1955). Such predictions are "predicted on the existence of persons like himself as *participants* within the system and not on the fatalistic view that the desired outcome is independent of the existence of such persons." There can be no compromise on such a vital point. Either we have history or we have myth. No half-way house is possible.

The classic frame of reference for contemporary theories of history derives from Vico, Condorcet and Lessing, and reached maturity in the work of Hegel. Indeed, the way history was used by Hegel, tended to undermine fears inherited from the French Enlightenment that history is basically a justification for tradition. In its place, new fears arose that history is basically a justification of revolution. But as empirical history developed, it tended to separate itself from philosophical history; the description of processes was seen as something quite apart from possible long-range values attached to historical events.

The first significant direct use of history in relation to sociology was made by Engels. In his writings on Hegel, Feuerbach and Dühring, Engels went far in showing the difference between a philosophical critique of society, and a sociological critique of philosophy involving distinctive attitudes to history. Engels' system of historical sociology rests on five variables, which may be tabulated as follows: (a) History distinguishes between ideological systems and the conscious deception by individuals; the former is a social question, the latter a problem of psychology. (b) There is a firm correlation of socio-economic foundations of a class and the ideology of that class. Historical changes in the former produce alterations in the latter. (c) An ideology is the historical necessity of class societies, and not simply the consequence of personality defects or power interests. (d) Ideologies are historically conditioned by the stage a society reaches in science, technology and culture, and further conditioned by national and regional peculiarities. (e) Economic interests are ultimately the source of all class projections, i.e., economy is as responsible for the production of ideas as it is of things. (Cf. Engels, 1885, 1886.) What Engels' historical sociology attempted to demonstrate was that ideology is part of a larger theory of ideas and not equivalent to knowledge as such. Ideology on such a view is a special condition of the social history of knowledge and the economic roots of social history.

The work of another follower in the Hegelian path, Mannheim, tended to weaken just this distinction between ideas and ideology. Nonetheless, Mannheim shared with Engels the attempt to create a secular, humanistic account of social and cultural history geared to yield results to problems which do not easily lend themselves to statistical or functional levels of analysis. A distinguished aspect of Mannheim's work was to reveal the specific historical position of intellectuals in past and present societies, and to show in addition that the principles of scientific socialism were themselves the product of intellectual currents with severe ideological limitations. Indeed, Mannheim was closer to the original Hegelian vision than to the Marxian version. The study of ideology became for Mannheim much more than the scientific study of the interrelation of interests and information. He went as far as equating the study of ideological thinking with "the history of the human mind" and "the perceptions of sociated persons." (Cf. Mannheim, 1956.) He became enmeshed in the very metaphysical preconceptions of history he originally attempted to explain.

The most outstanding shortcoming in historical sociology has been its inability to distinguish with any degree of clarity history as an empirical study from history as a philosophical undertaking to stake the field of what ought to be. The distinctions between truth and meaning were so blurred in the work of Hegel, Engels and Mannheim that it became difficult to study their historical work apart from studying the moral-political basis of how historical information was sifted and selected. Historical sociology has tended to lay claim to a more ultimate knowledge than is to be gained by other empirical disciplines. And it is just this insistence that has added fuel to the battle of the schools. The functionalist might not place such a premium on political and ethical neutrality if the historicist were a bit less convinced that truth cannot exist apart from meaning, and that the study of past history is the key to the future destinies of mankind.

To sum up the results of this chapter, we may say from a scientific position there is no objection to using various types of evidence in order to explain social events. To argue that the existence of a multiplicity of laws and levels in social theory would leave unresolved the ultimate problems of men, is not to take seriously the fact that mankind is not a discoverable essence but rather the general symbol for concrete men. Men have problems, not functional or historical abstractions. The validation and verification of data may rule out inspirational solutions to the "perennial" questions; but in breaking down monumental questions into manageable proportions, and in weeding out perennial nonsense from perennial questions. A scientific sociology resting on the integration of social levels, can do much to move beyond cosmic metaphysics. That philosophic predicates are involved in framing sociological laws is no argument against the existence of such laws, and just as assuredly no argument against the directive value of such laws.

In its own right, the sociology of knowledge has made a positive contribution in overcoming professional insularity and insolence in matters of communication and language by taking knowledge as a problem rather than as a heuristic given. It performs a further service of overcoming the private interests isolating philosophical studies from the behavioral and historical sciences. The sociology of knowledge offers a clear guide in measuring the extent to which extra-logical considerations enter into the formation of logically grounded methods of social explanation. More recently, the sociology of knowledge has pioneered in the relation of the intellectual to institutions of higher learning. (Cf. Znaniecki, 1940; Wilson, 1942; Lazarsfeld, 1958; Caplow and McGee, 1958; Dahlke, 1958.)

New areas of specialization are taking shape as scientific philosophy and the sociology of knowledge come to recognize that the study of the logic of language requires an appreciation of the sociological components of language. The measurement of such conceptual terms as democracy, ideology, objectivity, alienation, and authoritarianism requires a close union of the empirical tools of sociology and the analytical tools of logic and philosophy. Linguistic and logical analysis cuts across all levels of social existence; while the sociology of knowledge sheds light on many aspects of logical analysis; especially the social stimuli for such analysis. (Cf. Nettler, 1945, 1957; and Naess, 1956.) The growing interest in cross-disciplinary institutes, seminars on area problems and historical epochs, research in the simplification and unification of the language of social research, point to a wider basis of cooperation between sociology and philosophy than past generations thought either feasible or necessary.

The sociologist of knowledge and the philosopher of language must function as physician and clinician of ideas respectively. They should try to uncover the motives and reveal the consequences of idea-systems. Sociologists and philosophers can no more insist that their advice be taken than can the doctor or surgeon. But in the very process of informing men of their actual alternatives, if indeed alternatives are available, they can define the scope, limits and responsibilities of the scientific standpoint towards social reality.

Chapter X

Knowledge and Social Action

ONE of the root challenges of irrational philosophies to the scientific approach is that the latter has provided mankind with the tools of destroying the conditions of life it set out to improve. The irrationalist challenge declares that science has drawn us closer to the abyss from whence we came than to the tower of fresh human triumphs.

This oft-repeated indictment has the advantage of use rather than truth. Science as such can neither create nor destroy. This is the task of human agents. The function of modern science is to indicate the live options available to men, not to insist that one path alone will lead us to salvation. The invention of fire led to mass protection of men from the extremes of weather, and no less to the possibility of burning villages. The fashioning of stone and metal into tools laid the groundwork for the agricultural revolution, and no less the basis of armed warfare. The printing press created the possibility of a mass culture, and no less a humanity debauched by propaganda. Nuclear power, first used to destroy cities, can now be harnessed to replace conventional fuels. These commonplace examples of the alternative uses of science would become superfluous were men to realize that science is a social institution: social in origins, development, and uses.

The achievements of the physical sciences, the discovery of new sources of energy for either the enhancement or decimation of societies, place the social sciences in a position of having to intensify its own efforts to provide satisfactory solutions to problems of living. One of these tasks is to explain the role of science in society. For its part, the sociology of knowledge, in separating the realms of science and ideology, in uncovering the interest

130

elements motivating each, has been instrumental in providing a more mature framework for understanding the social basis of science. Central to its task has been extending the bounds of scientific inquiry to include the causal basis of social action and moral decision. The recent growth of a sociology of science, a sociology of education, the study of the social sources of technology and morals, all testify to the germinal role of the sociology of knowledge.

The point of view that we need a wider use of the behavioural sciences to indicate solutions to questions posed by the physical sciences has nothing in common with transforming science into a sacred cow, a new variety of fideism. The blunders made by even the best scientists, like Copernicus and Darwin, show how absurd such a position would be. The history of science simply indicates that the success of an enterprise is greater, and better able to mobilize public support, when and where established procedures of verification and confirmation are available.

The Nietzschean idea that scientific determinism destroys the human potential for moral action simply flies in the face of facts. But even were such an objection to science valid, there remains the question of what we mean by action. Do we desire action or accomplishment? In physics, work is defined in terms of the displacement or movement of an object rather than in terms of energy expended. If we stand by a wall for a day trying and failing to push it down, this does not constitute work in the physical sense. Whereas, if we harness natural energy and fashion an explosive to blow up the wall, this constitutes work. The social scientist can take a leaf from the physics textbooks. In social life also, it would be prudent to separate actual changes wrought in the human constellation from the sheer expenditure of physical and verbal energies. On this basis, science is the surest guide to moral action, for it best assures us that energy spent is transformed into changes registered. This is the advantage of scientific action over other forms of action. Science has furthermore changed the terms of the classic debate of whether determinism allows for action. The real question of moment is not the choice of action or inaction, but the instrumentalities and consequences of human energies.

Description by itself determines only the facts of a situation, but the meaning and value of facts require knowledge of the consequences of an action. The accurate description of an illness, be it personal or social, is but the first order of business for a science. The second order is to indicate the means presently available for overcoming an illness. The third, and highest order of business, is to search out new and improved means of treatment. The three orders of scientific business thus have a binding worth, a prescriptive value, that is quite different than a religious rite or a moral rule.

Of course, the prescriptive force of scientific statements are conditioned and constrained by the political, economic and cultural climate of the community. And it is here that the transition from the natural to the behavioural sciences is readily apparent. The rationalist belief in human life as a value to be preserved conditions social science in a unique way. For here alone values and human interests are as much factors of analysis as descriptions of processes. The political consequences of mass neurosis, the dangers inherent in an imbalance between industrial societies and underdeveloped agricultural areas, the threat to rational capital investment posed by an over-emphasis on consumption, these problems of the social sciences contain valuational considerations that must be accounted for. Because of this, social science is a filtering agent for intelligent social action, channelizing it along realizable goals.

Although the predictive capacities reached by each of the social sciences differ, none reveal a capricious universe. In most cases, the choice of action is limited and circumscribed by existing productive relations, political alignments, military power, etc. Human values are thus meaningful when they are grounded in knowledge of actual social alternatives. The uncovering of these realities does not end the search for higher ideals, but serves to make clear the difficulties involved in realizing such ideals. The imperfection of scientific knowledge, the admission that technonogical obstacles and ideological concerns condition many of the findings attained, is no argument against the practical implementation of its results. The realization of the partial nature of scientific discovery is no serious impediment to action. As an ancient Spanish proverb puts the matter: "'In the land of the blind, the one-eyed is king."

The growth of human societies indicates that there is sufficient scientific knowledge available to make real progress on the basis of it. We know enough to transform the basis of natural selection into a form of rational selection. However we wish to measure such advancement, whether in terms of the quantitative increase in population, the rise of urban civilizations, the lengthening of the life span, or in more involved terms of industrial and intellectual development, these are a direct consequence of social actions undertaken on a scientific basis. The investigation of the common needs and values that underlie human relations is a consequence of the realization that science includes man as an object for investigation no less than as the investigating object.

In the final analysis, the test of scientific propositions are in terms of their use in the practical, social life of man. The values of science are human values. The science of how values are formed itself rests on the idea that it is good to know the springs of action. The statement by Childe (1956) makes this point directly.

Major scientific discoveries of the greatest practical utility were indubitably made for precisely that motive without any reference to possible use. Yet the practical results, however long delayed, provide the sole conclusive test of the truth of the discovery, the proof that it is a contribution to knowledge and not just a new superstition. . . . I am not in the least perturbed if my description of Reality as a creative activity of process makes perfect knowledge and absolute truth unattainable. The function of knowledge is practical, to guide action. The success of the human species, the sole known society of knowers, in half a million years suffices to demonstrate that sufficient knowledge is attainable.

Rational action, goal-directed undertakings, is necessarily involved in indicating the short-run and long-run possibilities of success. Social science has the complicated task of indicating the price which must be paid for securing human wants. The separation of science from ideological and mythical thinking is made, not for the purpose of confining science to data gathering, but to make easier the social tasks of gaining ground on the unknown and the yet to be known. By doing this, social science helps create new values as well as further explicating old values. Scientific knowledge is one of the few forces now operating to unite man. Its distinction is a unique organization of knowledge so as to avoid a double theory of truth. The bifurcation of knowledge into possessors and seekers, and of society into myth creation and myth following, finds no place in a method which asserts the universality and communicability of its claims.

Scientific discovery is social in virtue of its intersubjective verification of all phenomena treated. When the tasks of science are coordinated with the needs of society as a whole, the possibility of harmonious growth is enhanced. The traditionalist fears of regimentation of knowledge under conditions of a controlled economy expressed by Polanyi (1951:ch.6) and Popper (1957: ch.21) does not face up to the technological realities of modern societies. The direction of investigations is already carefully circumscribed in every modern industrial society. The real question is not whether science includes a commitment to purposive behaviour, but the goals toward which scientific knowledge is directed. Taking as our standard our common human denominator, the preservation and extension of life, the goal of science is to maximize those opportunities which exist for furthering this standard. (Cf. Morgenthau, 1948:262.) This is the point at which science and human values show the greatest congruence.

If science is to be instrumental in securing social harmony, its findings must be respected, and its structural rigor acknowledged. When the methods and results of science become an accepted part of life, the existing anarchy and conflict of ideas, ideologies, and ideographs will be considerably lessened, if not eliminated. To expect the products of natural science and technology to accrue to men in common as long as morals are isolated from social science is to believe in myth not reason. Moral voluntarism sustains a theory of human behaviour as capricious and nature alone as subject to laws of change. The most urgent problem of this period is not the imagined imbalance between science and morality, technology and esthetics; these are simply cliches disguising the need for a more forthright deployment of the social sciences.

To reproach sociology for aping the methodologies of natural sciences is to quite miss the point of both the object and subject of sociological theory. What generally inspires criticism of the "deterministic" social sciences is a distaste for the rigorous practice these sciences commit men to. If conventionalist and phenomenalist theories of society are correct in asserting that science makes no claims to know the real nature of things and relations, but is simply a convenient way for ordering events, then these critics would be correct in asserting the need for extrascientific methods of analysis. If science has no more claim to truth than myth or ideology, then indeed all prescriptive statements would have to be declared to originate outside the sphere of rational activity and planning. On such grounds, science would be absolved from the uses made of its products. The physical scientist would have no need to learn the language of the social scientist. The anarchy of present-day national and international behaviour would be enshrined as a metaphysical verity, while the wailings of sociology would be attributed to an eccentric radicalism.

Three kinds of objectors to a scientific conception of society have become prominent within intellectual circles: philosophers who still remain convinced of the inherent metaphysical supremacy of their discipline in the study of human nature; natural scientists convinced that cosmic design is to nature what free will is to man; and those within the social sciences who see in societal patterns statistical regularities lacking any directional or prescriptive functions. Motivations differ in each kind of objector: the philosopher is fearful of losing his place as the historic interpreter of man, the natural scientist concerned with his privileged place in the academic community, the social scientist concerned over his historic associations with liberal and radical causes. The least commendable objectors to a scientific sociology are in the last category. In the rush for respectability, in the effort to convert sociology from a "dangerous" science to a "dismal" science, not a few sociologists have been willing to surrender any claim that the discipline extends to the search for explanation of human action based on social laws.

To these various lines of "inside" criticisms of social science many theoretical rejoinders have been offered. Yet only one kind of reply is completely satisfactory, skill and craft in applying the canons of science to urgent human issues. The mistake of the Enlightenment was to assume that the displacement of the unscientific by the scientific could proceed ideologically. But such an approach only raises the spectre of rationalistic dragons routing irrationalist demons; and the practice of social science can ill afford to conform to such caricature. "The social scientist, whose very object is the social world, can avoid studying the processes and problems of man in society only by pretending to be something he is not, or by lapsing into such a remote degree of abstraction or triviality as to make the resemblance between what he does and what he professes to be doing purely coincidental." (Cf. Wirth, 1954.)

In summing up the position of sociological theory, particularly the sociology of knowledge, and philosophic perspectives, I should like to dip into the vocabulary of the physician. Read (1953), in concluding his case for painless childbirth therapy, reveals the changed valuational climate of our age most forcefully.

Let your practice be founded upon the judgment of the intelligent, and your reputation upon honest opinion of those who are in the best position to judge. Above all, your own personal satisfaction will raise you to a different plane; your work will be in a different cause, you will not be numbered among the "Gehazis who seek only the shekels." Your belief is not in today, but rather tomorrow and those distant tomorrows which will bring man nearer to his ultimate heritage. Your faith is in the law of Nature; your science as adjutant and not as impediment to its implementation. Your shield and buckler will be hard work and quiet determination. Resolve to be patient, for by the results of your work you will be known. Men often value themselves by what they know they can do, forgetting that the world only values them by what they have done.

This combination of craft, creation and cooperation which characterizes science is the best solution to the afflictions which have long haunted men. It contrasts most sharply with the dominant

Hegelian emphasis of the last century, which thought of social change as catastrophic and painful. To be sure, catastrophe and pain may be no less facets of this age than of any other, but at least they have not been hypostatized as the sole means to great ends.

The attitude toward the sociology of knowledge and social theory developed in these pages is that a science of society is possible, which like painless childbirth obstetrics, makes possible a clearer understanding of the social machinery at work in the process of acquiring knowledge. As a result it can be instrumental in bringing about a more logical ordering of social relations than what we presently have, minus the pain and anguish that has attended the birth of new societies in the prescientific age. The function of knowledge is obviously to lessen the ordeals and anguish of life through control, and thus eliminate any further slaughter of the innocents. This ultimate function holds true for the birth of societies no less than for the birth of children.

Glossary of Terms

Several key terms have been employed in the text which deserve more elaborate definition. This is particularly the case for words not commonly used in the English language. I should just add a cautionary word: the definitions given aim at clarity rather than inclusiveness, and the list of terms selected only indicate a few of the linguistic difficulties in the sociology of knowledge and is not to be considered at all exhaustive. Below each definition is a book (or books) the reader can refer to for further elaboration.

Anomie—The atomization and disorganization characteristic of societies in flux (particularly industrial communities), which results in a loss of the feeling of social cohesion. As first used by Durkheim (1897), *anomie*, in contrast to egoism, fatalism and altruism, is a condition of deregulation and declassification. All advantages of social influence and ties are lost, and there is a drive for unattainable private goals. (Cf. Merton, 1938; Dohrenwend, 1959; Parsons, 1951a.)

Charisma—The definition of charisma and charismatic personality types most frequently encountered in sociological literature is that given by Weber (1947). It is "a certain quality of an individual personality by virtue of which he is set apart from ordinary men and treated as if endowed with supernatural, superhuman, or at least specifically exceptional powers or qualities. These are such as are not accessible to the ordinary person, but are regarded as of divine origin or as exemplary, and on the basis of them the individual concerned is treated as a leader." (Cf. Weber, 1919; Davies, 1954.)

Elite—That group of people who comprise the power holders of political or social institutions. The power holders include the leadership and the social formations from which leaders generally come, and to which accountability is maintained, during a given political era or a specific social generation. The elite does not include all members of a political institution, only those who partake in decision-making processes. (Cf. Michels, 1912; Pareto, 1916; and Lasswell, 1952.)

Geisteswissenschaften—The entire group of disciplines which have as their object establishing the independent level of reality occupied by historical, social and moral studies. What binds them together, and what is said to separate them from the natural sciences, is the necessity of taking into account in every social action the psychological qualities of man. This group of disciplines is further differentiated from the concept of the "cultural sciences" initiated by Rickert (1926) in that the *Geisteswissenschaften* specifically include the generalizing and explanatory social sciences. (Cf. Dilthey, 1922.)

Historicism—That tendency in the philosophy of history and in the sociology of knowledge which sees the truth of a proposition as bound to its changing historical position and the values of the historical moment. Historicism is often used to denote the resolution of the relationship of scientific knowledge and moral standards. As Meinecke explains it: "Each contains elements of the other in greater or less degree. Neither of these tendencies can be pursued one-sidedly; each needs the other to achieve its goal. What appears to be good for one is a path or signpost for the other. The search for causalities is one of these tendencies, the comprehension and exposition of values is the other. The search for causalities in history is impossible without reference to values; the comprehension of values is impossible without investigation of their causal origins." (Cf. Meinecke, 1933.)

Verifiability Principle—According to this principle, a sentence is empirically significant if and only if it is capable of complete verification by a logical deduction from some finite logically consistent set of observation sentences. These observation sentences need not be true, but they must be in a form which allows for their testability by potentially observable phenomena, that is, testable in principle. (Cf. Hempel, 1951.)

Weltanschauung—The totality of human interpretations of the world and of our life in the world (a problem of knowledge). At another level, it is the totality of the values by which men live (a problem of ethics). *Weltanschauung* is concerned with ultimate questions, with universal and general decisions. Thus the political, philosophical, or moral attitudes of an individual are only a part, a component element in his world view. (Cf. Sombart, 1939; Dilthey, 1927, 1931.)

Wissenssoziologie—The German word usually translated into English as the sociology of knowledge. The ambiguity in the translation resides in the much wider use the term "Wissen" has *vis-a-vis* the term "knowledge." Whereas the word "knowledge" is usually reserved for exact, scientific information, "Wissen" may have as its referential base such cultural phenomena as philosophic, religious and esthetic information. An additional ambiguity involved is that the German term carries with it not only greater scope but an indication of a higher truth value, i.e., metaphysical certainty. The English word knowledge is more carefully delineated to exclude non-verifiable information. Thus, while propaganda analysis, studies in mass culture, measurements in personal influence, etc. would all be included as part of *Wissenssoziologie,* they tend to form independent branches of study in non-German speaking areas. Clearly, these verbal distinctions have had extraverbal repercussions in the formation of a sociology of knowledge. All of which points to the increasing need for a common, unified language of the social sciences. (Cf. Maquet, 1949; and Wolff, 1959.)

Bibliographical References

Abel, T. (1948): The Operation Called *Verstehen. Am. J. Sociology,* Vol. 54, 1948.

Adler, F. (1954): *A Quantitative Study in the Sociology of Knowledge.* Department of Sociology, University of Arkansas, Fayetteville, Arkansas. Mimeographed copy, privately distributed.

Adler, F. (1957): The Range of Sociology of Knowledge, in *Modern Sociological Theory in Continuity and Change,* ed. Becker and Boskoff. New York, Dryden Press, 1957.

Adorno, T. N. (ed.) (1950): *The Authoritarian Personality,* Studies in Prejudice Series. New York, Harper & Bros., 1950.

Anderson F. (1948): *The Philosophy of Francis Bacon.* Chicago, University of Chicago Press, 1948.

Aron, R. (1935): *German Sociology.* Glencoe, The Free Press, 1957.

Ayer, A. J. (1936): *Language, Truth and Logic.* New York, Dover Press, 1946.

Bachelard, G. (1957): *La Formation de l'esprit scientifique: contribution a une psychoanalyse de la connaissance objective.* Paris, J. Vrin, 1957.

Bacon, F. (1620): *Novum Organum, or True Directions Concerning The Interpretation of Nature,* in *The English Philosophers From Bacon to Mill,* ed. E. A. Burtt. New York, Random House, 1939.

Barth, H. (1945): *Wahrheit und Ideologie.* Zurich, Manesse Verlag, 1945.

Barth, K. (1926): *Die Theologie und die Kirche.* Zurich, Evangelischer Verlag, 1928.

Barth, P. (1922): Die ideologische Geschichtsauffassung, in *Die Philosophie der Geschichte als Soziologie.* Leipzig, O. R. Reisland, 1922.

Barzun, J. (1941): After Marx, What Is Social Science? in *Darwin, Marx, Wagner: Critique of a Heritage* (revised second edition). New York, Doubleday & Co., 1958.

Becker, H. and Barnes, H. E. (1952): *Social Thought From Lore To Science.* Washington, D. C., Harren Press, 1952.

Bendix, R. (1954): Social Theory and Social Action in the Sociology of Louis Wirth, in *Am. J. Sociology,* Vol. 59, 1954.

Benedict, R. (1953): Continuities and Discontinuities in Cultural Conditioning, in *Personality in Nature, Society and Culture,* ed. Kluckhohn, Murray, Schneider. New York, Alfred Knopf, 1953.

Berelson, B. (1951): *Content Analysis in Communications Research.* Glencoe, The Free Press, 1951.

Berelson, B. (1952): Democratic Theory and Public Opinion. *Public Opinion Quarterly,* Vol. XVI, 1952.

Bergmann, G. (1951): Ideology. *Ethics,* Vol. 61, 1951.

Berlin, I. (1954): *Historical Inevitability.* London and New York, Oxford University Press, 1955.

Bernal, J. D. (1954): The Social Sciences in History, in *Science in History.* London, Watts & Co., 1954.

Bloch, E. (1946): *Freiheit und Ordnung, Abriss der Sozial-Utopien.* Aurora Verlag, New York, 1946.

Bloomfield, L. (1955): *Linguistic Aspects of Science. International Encyclopedia of Unified Science,* Vol. I, No. 4 (combined edition). Chicago, University of Chicago Press, 1955.

Bodde, D. (1957): *China's Cultural Tradition.* New York, Rinehart & Co., 1957.

Bogardus, E. S. (1940): Chinese Social Thought, in *The Development of Social Thought.* New York and London, Longmans, Green & Co., 1940.

Braithwaite, R. B. (1953): *Scientific Explanation: A Study of the Function of Theory, Probability and Laws in Science.* Cambridge, Cambridge University Press, 1953.

Brill, A. A. (1949): *Basic Principles of Psychoanalysis.* New York, Doubleday & Co., Inc., 1949.

Brodbeck, M. (1959): Models, Meaning and Theories, in *Symposium on Sociological Theory,* ed. Llewellyn Gross. Evanston and White Plains, Row, Peterson & Co., 1959.

Brown, N. O. (1959): The Protestant Era, in *Life Against Death, the Psychoanalytical Meaning of History.* Middletown, Wesleyan University, 1959.

Bukharin, N. I. (1935): Marx's Teaching and Its Historical Importance, in *Marxism and Modern Thought,* ed. Ralph Fox. London, George Routledge & Sons, 1935.

Bunge, M. (1959): *Causality: The Place of the Causal Principle in Modern Science.* Cambridge, Harvard University Press, 1959.

Butterfield, H. (1949): *The Origins of Modern Science, 1300-1800.* London, G. Bell, Ltd., 1949.

Campanella, T. (1623): Civitas Solis, idea reipublicae Platonicae, in *Famous Utopias of the Renaissance,* ed. F. R. White. New York, Packard & Co., 1946.

Cantril, H. A. (1940): *The Invasion From Mars.* Princeton, Princeton University Press, 1940.

Cantril, H. A. (1950): Projective Questions in the Study of Personality and Ideology, in *The Authoritarian Personality,* loc. cit.

Caplow, T., and McGee, R. J. (1958): *The Academic Marketplace.* New York, Basic Books, Inc., 1958.

Carnap, R. (1937): *The Logical Syntax of Language,* London, Routledge & Kegan Paul, Ltd., 1949.

Cassirer, E. (1946): *The Myth of the State.* New Haven, Yale University Press, 1946.

Child, A. H. (1938): *The Problem of the Sociology of Knowledge: A Critical and Philosophical Study.* Unpublished Ph.D. dissertation. University of California, Berkeley, California, 1938.

Child, A. H. (1941): The Theoretical Possibility of the Sociology of Knowledge. *Ethics,* Vol. 51, 1941.

Child, A. H. (1947): The Problem of Truth in the Sociology of Knowledge. *Ethics,* Vol. 58, 1947.

Childe, V. G. (1936): *Man Makes Himself.* London, Watts & Co., 1948.

Childe, V. G. (1949): The Sociology of Knowledge. *The Modern Quarterly,* Vol. 5, 1949.

Childe, V. G. (1956): *Society and Knowledge.* New York, Harper & Bros., 1956.

Christie, R. and Jahoda, M. (Eds.) (1954): *Studies in the Scope and Method of The Authoritarian Personality.* Glencoe, The Free Press, 1954.

Chuang-Tzu (1939): Autumn Floods, in *Three Ways of Thought in Ancient China,* ed. Arthur Waley. New York, Doubleday & Co., 1956.

Cohen, R. S. (1954): Alternative Interpretations of the History of Science, in *The Validation of Scientific Theories,* ed. Philipp G. Frank. Boston, The Beacon Press, 1956.

Cohen, R. S. (1960): Dialectical Materialism and Carnap's Logical Empiricism, in *The Philosophy of Rudolph Carnap. The Library of Living Philosophers,* Vol. XI, ed. Paul A. Schilpp. New York, Wiley Book Co., 1961. (Publication pending)

Comte, A. (1853): *Positive Philosophy (Cours de philosophie positive),* trans. Harriet Martineau. London, Kegan Paul, 1893.

Cornford, F. M. (1950): *The Unwritten Philosophy and Other Essays.* Cambridge, Cambridge University Press, 1950.

Dahlke, H. O. (1940): The Sociology of Knowledge, in *Contemporary Social Theory,* ed. Barnes and Becker. New York and London, D. Appleton Co., 1940.

Dahlke, H. O. (1958): *Values in Culture and Classroom: A Study in the Sociology of the School.* New York, Harper & Bros., 1958.

Dahrendorf, R. (1958): Out of Utopia: Toward a Reorganization of Sociological Analysis. *Am. J. Sociology,* Vol. 64, 1958.

Dantzig, D. V. (1951): The Function of Words in Ideological Conflicts, in *Democracy in a World of Tensions,* ed. Richard McKeon. Chicago, University of Chicago Press, 1951.

Davies, J. C. (1954): Charisma in the 1952 Campaign. *The American Political Science Review*, Vol. 48, 1954.

Davis, A. K. (1957): Social Theory and Social Problems: Fragments For A Philosophy of Social Science. *Philosophy and Phenomenological Research*, Vol. 18, 1957.

DeGré, G. L. (1943): *Society and Ideology: An Inquiry into the Sociology of Knowledge*. New York, Privately Printed, 1943.

DeGré, G. L. (1955): *Science as a Social Institution*. New York, Doubleday & Co., 1955.

de Tracy, D. (1801): *Eléments d'idéologie*. Brussels (Belgium), 1826.

Dewey, J. (1929): *The Quest For Certainty*. Minton, Balch & Co., New York, 1929.

Dewey, J. (1938): Logic: *The Theory of Inquiry*. New York, Henry Holt & Co., 1938.

Dewey, J. (1939): *Freedom and Culture*. New York, G. P. Putnam's Sons, 1939.

Dewey, J. (1944): Antinaturalism in Extremis, in *Naturalism and the Human Spirit*, ed. Y. H. Krikorian. New York, Columbia University Press, 1944.

Dilthey, W. (1905): Studie zur Grundlegung der Geisteswissenschaften, in *Der Aufbau der geschichtlichen Welt in den Geisteswissenschaften, Gesammelte Schriften*, Vol. VII. Leipzig and Berlin, B. G. Teubner, 1927.

Dilthey, W. (1921): *Die Jugendgeschichte Hegels und andere Abhandlungen zur Geschichte des deutschen Idealismus. Gesammelte Schriften*, Vol. IV. Leipzig and Berlin, B. G. Teubner, 1921.

Dilthey, W. (1922): *Einleitung in die Geisteswissenschaften. Gesammelte Schriften*, Vol. I. Leipzig and Berlin, B. G. Teubner, 1922.

Dilthey, W. (1924): Das Wesen der Philosophie, in *Die geistige Welt. Gesammelte Schriften*, Vol. V. Leipzig and Berlin, B. G. Teubner, 1924.

Dilthey, W. (1927): Das geschichtliche Bewusstsein und die Weltanschauungen, in *Studien zur Geschichte des deutschen Geistes, Gesammelte Schriften*, Vol. III. Leipzig and Berlin, B. G. Teubner, 1927.

Dilthey, W. (1931): Die Typen der Weltanschauung und ihre Ausbildung in den metapyhisischen Systemen, in *Weltanschauungslehre. Gesammelte Schriften*, Vol. VIII. Leipzig and Berlin, B. G. Teubner, 1931.

Dohrenwend, B. P. (1959): Egoism, Altruism, Anomie, and Fatalism: A Conceptual Analysis of Durkheim's Types, *Am. Sociological Review*, Vol. 24, 1959.

Dostoevsky, F. M. (1864): *Notes From Underground*, in *Existentialism from Dostoevsky to Sartre*, ed. Walter Kaufman. New York, Meridian Books, 1956.

Duncan, H. D. (1953): *Language and Literature in Society*. Chicago, The University of Chicago Press, 1953.

Durkheim, E. (1893): *The Division of Labor in Society,* trans. George Simpson. New York, The Macmillan Co., 1933.

Durkheim, E. (1895): *The Rules of Sociological Method.* Chicago, The University of Chicago Press, 1938.

Durkheim, E. (1897): Suicide, *A Study in Sociology.* Glencoe, The Free Press, 1951.

Durkheim, E. (1912): *The Elementary Forms of the Religious Life, A Study in Religious Sociology,* trans. Joseph W. Swain. London, George Allen & Unwin, Ltd., 1915.

Durkheim, E. (1924): *Sociology and Philosophy,* trans. D. F. Pocock. Glencoe, The Free Press, 1951.

Duverger, M. (1951): *Les Partis Politiques.* Paris, Librairie Armand Colin, 1951.

Edel, A. (1949): Context and Content in the Theory of Ideas, in *Philosophy for the Future,* ed. Sellars, Farber, McGill. New York, The Macmillan Co., 1949.

Edel, A. (1955): *Ethical Judgment: The Use of Science in Ethics.* Glencoe, The Free Press, 1955.

Edel, A. (1959a): The Concept of Levels in Social Theory, in *Symposium on Sociological Theory,* ed. Llewellyn Gross. *loc.cit.*

Edel, A. and Edel M. (1959b): *Anthropology and Ethics* (American Lecture Series). Springfield, Thomas, 1959.

Eliade, M. (1958): The Structure and Morphology of the Sacred, in *Patterns in Comparative Religion.* New York, Sheed & Ward, 1958.

Engels, F. (1872-82): *Dialectics of Nature,* ed. Clemens Dutt. New York, International Publishers, 1940.

Engels, F. (1880): *Socialism: Utopian and Scientific.* New York, International Publishers, 1935.

Engels, F. (1885): *Herr Eugen Dühring's Revolution in Science (Anti-Dühring).* New York, International Publishers, 1939.

Engels, F. (1886): *Ludwig Feuerbach and the Outcome of Classical German Philosophy.* New York, International Publishers, 1941.

Engels, F. (1894): On The History of Early Christianity, in *Marx and Engels on Religion.* Moscow, Foreign Languages Publishing House, 1957.

Farber, M. (1956): *Husserl.* Buenos Aires, Ediciones Losange, 1956,

Farrington, B. (1939): *Science and Politics in the Ancient World.* London, George Allen & Unwin, 1939.

Farrington, B. (1949): *Francis Bacon, Philosopher of Industrial Science.* New York, Henry Schuman & Co., 1949.

Fenichel, O. (1927): The Economic Function of Screen Memories, in *The Collected Papers of Otto Fenichel,* Vol. I, ed. F. Fenichel and D. Rapaport. New York, W. W. Norton & Co., 1953.

Festinger, L. and Katz, D. (1953): *Research Methods in the Behavioral Sciences.* New York, The Dryden Press, 1953.

Feuerbach, L. (1841): *The Essence of Christianity,* trans. George Eliot. New York, Harper & Bros., 1957.

Frank, P. (1952): Contributions to the Analysis and Synthesis of Knowledge, in *Proceedings of the American Academy of Arts and Sciences,* Vol. 80, No. 2, 1952.

Frankel, C. (1955): Can History Tell the Truth? in *The Case for Modern Man.* New York, Harper & Bros., 1955.

Freud, S. (1908): The Relation of the Poet to Day-Dreaming, in *Collected Papers,* Vol. IV. London, Hogarth Press Ltd., 1925.

Freud, S. (1917): *Psychopathology of Everyday Life. New York,* Macmillan Co., 1948.

Freud, S. (1930): *Civilization and Its Discontents.* New York, Cape & Smith, 1930.

Freyer, H. (1928): The Problem of Utopia, in *Deutsche Rundschau,* Vol. 183, 1928.

Freyer, H. (1930): Anmerkungen über das Problem der Ideologie und über Wissenssoziologie, in *Soziologie als Wirklichkeitswissenschaft, logische Grundlegung des Systems der Soziologie.* Leipzig and Berlin, B. G. Teubner, 1930.

Fried, E. (1942): Techniques of Persuasion, in *Propaganda by Short Wave,* ed. Harwood Childs and John Whitton. Princeton, Princeton University Press, 1942.

Fromm, E. (1941): *Escape from Freedom.* New York, Farrar & Rinehart, 1941.

Fromm, E. (1947): *Man for Himself: An Inquiry into the Psychology of Ethics.* New York, Rinehart & Co., 1947.

Fromm, E. (1955): *The Sane Society.* New York, Rinehart & Co., 1955.

Galbraith, J. K. (1958): *The Affluent Society.* Boston, Houghton-Mifflin Co., 1958.

Germani, G. (1955a): *Estudios de Psicología Social,* Mexico, D.F., Biblioteca de Ensayos Sociológicos, Instituto de Investigaciones Sociales, Universidad Nacional, 1955.

Germani, G. (1955b): *La Sociología Científica* (Cuadernos de Sociología), Mexico, D.F., Biblioteca de Ensayos Sociológicos, Instituto de Investigaciones Sociales, Universidad Nacional, 1955.

Gillin, J. (1954): *For a Science of Social Man: Convergences in Anthropology, Psychology, and Sociology.* New York, Macmillan Co., 1954.

Ginsberg, M. (1948): *Reason and Unreason in Society: Essays in Sociology and Social Philosophy.* Cambridge, Harvard University Press, 1948.

Gittler, J. B. (1940): Possibilities of a Sociology of Sciences, in *Social Forces*, Vol. 18, 1940.

Gottfried, A. (1955): The Use of Socio-Psychological Categories in a Study of Political Personality, in *The Western Political Quarterly*, Vol. 8, 1955.

Gottlieb, M. (1953): The Theory of an Economic System, in *The American Economic Review*, Vol. 43, 1953.

Gouldner, A. W. (1959): Reciprocity and Autonomy in Functional Theory, in *Symposium on Sociological Theory*, ed. Llewellyn Gross. *Loc. cit.*

Greenberg, J. H. (1959): An Axiomatization of the Phonologic Aspect of Language, in *Symposium on Sociological Theory*, ed. Llewellyn Gross. *Loc.cit.*

Grinker, R. R. (ed.): *Toward a Unified Theory of Human Behavior*. New York, Basic Books, 1956.

Groethuysen, B. (1913): Wilhelm Dilthey, in *Deutsche Rundschau*, Vol. 154, 1913.

Groethuysen, B. (1927): *Die Entstehung der bürgerlichen Welt und Lebensanschauung in Frankreich (Philosophie und Geisteswissenschaften*, Vol. 4), Halle, M. Niemeyer, 1927.

Gross, F. (ed.) *European Ideologies: A Survey of Twentieth Century Political Ideas*. New York, Philosophical Library, 1948.

Grünbaum, A. (1953): Causality and the Science of Human Behavior, in *Readings in the Philosophy of Science*, ed. H. Feigl and M. Brodbeck. New York, Appleton-Century-Crofts Co., 1953.

Grünbaum, A. (1955): Time and Entropy, in *Am. Scientist*, Vol. 43, 1955.

Grünbaum, A. (1960): Carnap's Views on the Foundations of Geometry, in *The Philosophy of Rudolph Carnap. The Library of Living Philosophers*, Vol. XI, ed. Paul A. Schilpp. New York, Wiley Book Co., 1961. (Publication pending.)

Grünwald, E. (1934): *Das Problem der Soziologie des Wissens*. Wien and Leipzig, Universitäts-Verlagsbuchhandlung, 1934.

Gumplowicz, L. (1899): Concept, Function, Scope and Importance of Sociology, in *The Outlines of Sociology*. Philadelphia, American Academy of Political and Social Science, 1899.

Gurvitch, G. (1955): *Trois Chapitres d'Histoire de la Sociologie: Auguste Comte, Karl Marx et Herbert Spencer*, Paris, Centre de Documentation Universitaire, 1955.

Gurvitch, G. (1957): Reflections on the Relationship Between Philosophy and Sociology, *Cahiers Internationaux de Sociologie*, Vol. 22, 1957.

Gurvitch, G. (1957-59): Le problème de la Sociologie de la Connaissance. *Revue Philosophique*, Vol. 147, 1957; Vol. 148, 1958; Vol. 149, 1959.

Halbwachs, M. (1935): La mémoire collective Réligieuse, in *Les Cadres Sociaux de la Mémiore*. Paris, Librairie Félix Alcan, 1935.

Hare, R. M. (1952): *The Language of Morals.* Oxford, The Clarendon Press, 1952.

Hauser, A. (1951): *The Social History of Art* (2 vols.). New York, Alfred A. Knopf, 1951.

Hauser, A. (1959): *The Philosophy of Art History.* New York, Alfred A. Knopf, 1959.

Hegel, G. W. F. (1807): *Phenomenology of Mind,* trans. J. B. Baillie. London, Oxford University Press, 1931.

Hegel, G. W. F. (1812): *Science of Logic* (2 vols.), trans. W. H. Johnston and L. G. Struthers. New York, The Macmillan Co., 1929.

Hegel, G. W. F. (1820): *Philosophy of Right,* trans. T. M. Knox. London, Oxford University Press, 1945.

Hegel, G. W. F. (1833-36): *Lectures on the History of Philosophy* (3 vols.), trans. E. S. Haldane. London, Routledge & Kegan Paul, Ltd., 1955.

Hegel, G. W. F. (1837): *The Philosophy of History,* trans. J. Sibree. New York, Willey Book Co., 1944.

Heidegger, M. (1929): *Was ist Metaphysik?* in *Existence and Being.* Chicago, Henry Regnery Co., 1949.

Helmer, O. and Rescher, N. (1959): On the Epistemology of the Inexact Sciences. *Management Science,* Vol. 6, 1959.

Helvetius, C. A. (1758): *Essays on the Mind (De l'Esprit),* London, 1809.

Helvetius, C. A. (1772): *A Treatise on Man, His Intellectual Faculties and His Education (De l'Homme).* London, 1810.

Hempel, C. G. (1942): The Function of General Laws in History. *J. Philosophy,* Vol. 39, 1942.

Hempel, C. G. and Oppenheim, P. (1948): Studies in the Logic of Explanation. *Philosophy of Science,* Vol. 15, 1948.

Hempel, C. G. (1951): The Concept of Cognitive Significance: A Reconsideration," in *Contributions to the Analysis and Synthesis of Knowledge. Proceedings of the A.A.A.S.,* Vol. 80, No. 1, 1951.

Hempel, C. G. (1959): The Logic of Functional Analysis, in *Symposium on Sociological Theory,* ed. Llewellyn Gross. *Loc. cit.*

Herrick, C. J. (1949): A Biological Survey of Integrative Levels, in *Philosophy for the Future,* ed. Sellars, Farber, McGill. *Loc. cit.* (See reference to Alex B. Novikoff, *Science,* Vol. 101, 1945.)

Hinshaw, V. G. (1943): The Epistemological Relevance of Mannheim's Sociology of Knowledge. *J. Philosophy,* Vol. 40, 1943.

Hodges, H. A. (1944): *Wilhelm Dilthey: An Introduction.* London, Routledge & Kegan Paul, Ltd., 1944.

Hodges, H. A. (1952): *The Philosophy of Wilhelm Dilthey*. London, Routledge & Kegan Paul, Ltd., 1952.

Hoffer, E. (1951): *The True Believer: Thoughts on the Nature of Mass Movements*. New York, Harper & Bros., 1951.

Honigsheim, P. (1924): Die Gegenwartskrise der Kulturinstitute in ihrer soziologischen Bedingtheit; and Stileinheit zwischen Wirtschaft und Geisteskultur, in *Versuche zu einer Soziologie des Wissens*, ed. Max Scheler. Munich, Duncker & Humblot, 1924.

Honigsheim, P. (1950): Max Weber: His Religious and Ethical Background and Development, in *Church History*. Vol. XIX, 1950.

Honigsheim, P. (1958): Religionssoziologie, in *Die Lehre von der Gesellschaft*, ed. Gottfried Eisermann. Stuttgart, Ferdinand Enke Verlag, 1958.

Horkheimer, M. (1939): The Relation Between Psychology and Sociology in the Work of Wilhelm Dilthey, in *Studies in Philosophy and Sociology (Zeitschrift für Sozialforschung)*, Vol. VIII, No. 3, 1939.

Horney, K. (1937): *The Neurotic Personality of Our Time*. New York, W. W. Norton & Co., 1937.

Horowitz, I. L. (1957a): *The Idea of War and Peace in Contemporary Philosophy*. New York, Paine-Whitman, 1957.

Horowitz, I. L. (1957b): German Marxism: Renaissance and Repression. *Dissent*, Vol. IV, 1957.

Horowitz, I. L. (1958a): The Moral and the Ethical. *Philosophy & Phenomenological Research*, Vol. 19, 1958.

Horowitz, I. L. and Joynt, C. B. (1958b): Toynbee, Sociedad y Conocimiento. *Boletín del Instituto de Sociología, Facultad de Filosofía y Letras de la Universidad de Buenos Aires*, Vol. XI, No. 12, 1958.

Horowitz, I. L. (1958c): Edgar Zilsel: una apreciacion retrospectiva. *Boletín del Instituto de Sociología, Facultad de Filosofía y Letras de la Universidad de Buenos Aires*, Vol. XI, No. 11, 1958.

Horowitz, I. L. (1961): *Radicalism and the Revolt Against Reason: The Social Theories of Georges Sorel*. London, Routledge & Kegan Paul, Ltd., 1961.

Hume, D. (1757): *The Natural History of Religion*. London, Adam and Charles Black, 1956.

James, W. (1907): *Pragmatism and Four Essays from "The Meaning of Truth."* New York, Longmans, Green & Co., 1943.

Jaspers, K. (1955): *Reason and Existenz*. New York, The Noonday Press, 1955.

Jerusalem, W. J. (1821): Soziologie des Erkennens, in *Kölner Vierteljahrshefte für Sozialwissenschaften*, Vol. I, 1921.

Joynt, C. B. (1956): Toynbee and Historical Knowledge. *Australian J. of Philosophy*, Vol. 34, 1956.

Kant, I. (1781): *The Critique of Pure Reason,* trans. Max Müller. New York, The Macmillan Co., 1927.

Kardiner, A. (1949): Psychodynamics and the Social Sciences, in *Culture and Personality,* ed. S. Stansfeld Sargent and Marian W. Smith. New York, Werner-Gren Foundation for Anthropological Research, Inc., 1949.

Kaufman, F. (1944): *Methodology of the Social Sciences.* London and New York, Oxford University Press, 1944.

Kelsen, H. (1943): *Society and Nature: A Sociological Enquiry.* Chicago, The University of Chicago Press, 1943.

Kelsen, H. (1955): *The Communist Theory of Law.* New York, Praeger, 1955.

Labedz, L. (1958): The Soviet Attitude to Sociology, in *The Soviet Cultural Scene: 1956-1957,* ed. W. Z. Laquer and George Lichtheim. New York, Atlantic Books-Praeger, 1958.

Landsberg, P. (1931): Zur Soziologie der Erkenntnistheorie, in *Schmollers Jahrbuch für Gesetzgebung, Verwaltung und Volkswirtschaft,* 1931.

Lasswell, H. D. (1930): *Psychopathology and Politics.* Chicago, The University of Chicago Press, 1930.

Lasswell, H. D. *et al.* (1946): *Propaganda, Communication, and Public Opinion: A Comprehensive Reference Guide.* Princeton, Princeton University Press, 1946.

Lasswell, H. D., *et al* (1952): *The Comparative Study of Elites: An Introduction and Bibliography,* (Hoover Institute Studies: Series B). Stanford, Stanford University Press, 1952.

Latham, R (1951): Introduction to *On the Nature of the Universe* (Lucretius). Harmondsworth-Middlesex, Penguin Books, 1951.

Lavine, T. Z. (1944): Naturalism and the Sociological Analysis of Knowledge, in *Naturalism and the Human Spirit,* ed. Y. H. Krikorian. New York, Columbia University Press. 1944.

Lazarsfeld, P. F. (ed.) (1954): Introduction, in *Mathematical Thinking in the Social Sciences.* Glencoe, The Free Press, 1954.

Lazarsfeld, P. F. and Katz, E. (1955): *Personal Influence: The Part Played by People in the Flow of Mass Communications,* Glencoe, The Free Press, 1955.

Lazarsfeld, P. F. and Thielens, W. (1958): *The Academic Mind.* Glencoe, The Free Press, 1958.

Lee, O. (1949): *Existence and Inquiry: A Study of Thought in the Modern World.* Chicago, The University of Chicago Press, 1949.

Lefebvre, H. (1947): *Logique Formelle, Logique Dialectique (À la lumière du matérialisme dialectique,* Vol. I). Paris, Éditions Sociales, 1947.

Lenin, V. I. (1908): *Materialism and Empirio-Criticism: Critical Comments on a Reactionary Philosophy*. Moscow, Foreign Language Publishing House, 1947.

Lenin, V. I. (1922): Transition from Capitalism to Communism, in *Marx-Engels-Marxism*. New York, International Publishers, 1935.

Lenzen, V. F. (1954): *Causality in Natural Science* (American Lecture Series). Springfield, Thomas, 1954.

Lenzen, V. F. (1955): *Procedures of Empirical Science*. International Encyclopedia of Unified Science, Vol. I, No. 5, 1955. (combined edition)

Levinson, D. J. (1950): The Study of Ethnocentric Ideology, in *The Authoritarian Personality*, ed. Adorno and associates. *Loc. cit.*

Levinson, R. (1953): *In Defense of Plato*. Cambridge, Harvard University Press, 1953.

Lévy-Bruhl, L. (1899): *History of Modern Philosophy in France*. Chicago, The Open Court Publishing Co., 1899.

Lévy-Bruhl, L. (1922): *Primitive Mentality*. New York, The Macmillan Co., 1923.

Lewin, K. (1917): Die Psychische Tätigkeit bei der Hemmung von Willensorgängen und das Grundgesetz der Assoziation, in *Zeitschrift für Psychologie*, Vol. 77, 1917.

Lewin, K. (1948): The Field Theory Level of Social Science, in *Resolving Social Conflicts*. New York, Harper & Bros., 1948.

Lewin, K. (1951): Defining the Field at a Given Time, in *Field Theory in Social Science*. New York, Harper & Bros., 1951.

Lewis, J. (1957): Idealism and Ideologies, in *Marxism and the Open Mind*. New York, Paine-Whitman, 1957.

Likert, R. and Lippitt, R. (1953): The Utilization of Social Science, in *Research Methods in the Behavioral Sciences*, ed. Festinger and Katz. New York, The Dryden Press, 1953.

Lipset, S. M. (1959): Political Sociology, in *Sociology Today, Problems and Prospects*, ed. Merton, Broom, and Cottrell. New York, Basic Books, Inc., 1959.

Liu Shao (1937): *Jen Wu Chih*, in *The Study of Human Abilities*. New Haven, American Oriental Society, 1937.

Lowenthal, L. (1932): Zur gesellschaftlichen Lage der Literatur, in *Zeitschrift für Sozialforschung*, Vol. I, 1932.

Lowenthal, L. (1957): *Literature and the Image of Man: Sociological Studies of the European Drama and Novel, 1600-1900*. Boston, The Beacon Press, 1957.

Lucretius Carus (1951): *On the Nature of the Universe*, trans. R. Latham. Harmondsworth-Middlesex, Penguin Books, 1951.

Lukacs, G. (1923): *Geschichte und Klassenbewusstsein: Studien über marxistische Dialektik*. Berlin, Malik Verlag, 1923.

Lukacs, G. (1948a): Théorie Léninienne de la Connaissance et les problèmes de la philosophie moderne, in *Existentialisme ou Marxisme?* Paris, Editions Nagel, 1948.

Lukacs, G. (1948b): Marx und das Problem des ideologischen Verfalls, in *Karl Marx und Friedrich Engels als Literaturhistoriker.* Berlin, Aufbau Verlag, 1948.

Lukacs, G. (1950): *Studies in European Realism: A Sociological Survey of the Writings of Balzac, Stendhal, Zola, Tolstoy, Gorki, and others.* London, Hillway Publishing Co., 1950.

Lukacs, G. (1953): *Die Zerstörung der Vernunft.* Berlin, Aufbau-Verlag, 1953.

Lundberg, G. A. (1947): *Can Science Save Us?* New York, Longmans, Green & Co., 1947.

Lützeler, H. (1932): Problem der Literatursoziologie, in *Die Neuere Sprache,* Vol. 40, 1932.

Malebranche, N. (1674): *De la recherche de la vérité* (English translation). London, 1694.

Malinowski, B. (1948): *Magic, Science and Religion, and other essays.* Boston, The Beacon Press, 1948.

Mandelbaum, M. (1938): *The Problem of Historical Knowledge.* New York, Liveright Publishing Co., 1938.

Mandelbaum, M. (1955): *The Phenomenology of Moral Experience.* Glencoe, The Free Press, 1955.

Mannheim, K. (1929): *Ideology and Utopia.* New York, Harcourt, Brace & Co., 1936.

Mannheim, K. (1935): *Man and Society in an Age of Reconstruction.* New York, Harcourt, Brace & Co., 1940.

Mannheim, K. (1953): *Essays on Sociology and Social Psychology,* ed. Paul Kecskemeti. London, Routledge & Kegan Paul, Ltd., 1953.

Mannheim, K. (1956): *Essays on the Sociology of Culture.* London, Routledge & Kegan Paul, Ltd., 1956.

Maquet, J. J. (1949): *The Sociology of Knowledge, Its Structure and its Relation to the Philosophy of Knowledge, A Critical Analysis of the Systems of Karl Mannheim and Pitirim A. Sorokin,* trans. J. F. Locke. Boston, The Beacon Press, 1951.

Marcuse, H. (1929): Zur Wahrheitsproblematik der soziologischen Methode Karl Mannheims Ideologie und Utopie, *Die Gesellschaft,* Vol. 6, 1929.

Marcuse, H. (1941): *Reason and Revolution: Hegel and the Rise of Social Theory.* New York, Oxford University Press, 1941.

Marcuse, H. (1955): *Eros and Civilization: A Philosophical Inquiry Into Freud.* Boston, The Beacon Press, 1955.

Maritain, J. (1951): The Problem of World Government, in *Man and the State*. Chicago, The University of Chicago Press, 1951.

Marquis, D. G. (1948): Scientific Methodology in Human Relations, in *Proceedings of the American Philosophical Society*, Vol. XCII, 1948.

Martindale, D. (1959): Sociological Theory and the Ideal Type, in *Symposium on Sociological Theory*, ed. Llewellyn Gross. *Loc. cit.*

Marx, K. (1844): *Economic and Philosophic Manuscripts of 1844*, trans. M. Milligan. Moscow, Foreign Languages Publishing House, 1957.

Marx, K. and Engels, F. (1845): *The Holy Family, or Critique of Critical Critique*. Moscow, Foreign Languages Publishing House, 1956,

Marx, K. and Engels, F. (1846): *The German Ideology*, ed. Roy Pascal. New York, International Publishers, 1939.

Marx, K. (1847): *The Poverty of Philosophy*. Moscow, Foreign Languages Publishing House, 1956.

Marx, K. (1859): *A Contribution to the Critique of Political Economy*. Chicago, Charles Kerr Co., 1904.

Marx, K. (1867): *Capital: A Critique of Political Economy* (Vol. I, *The Process of Capitalist Production*). Chicago, Charles Kerr Co., 1909.

Mayer, J. P. (1944): *Max Weber and German Politics: A Study of Political Sociology*. London, Faber & Feber, 1944.

McGlynn, J. V. (1958): A Note on Philosophy in German Universities Today, in *Philosophy and Phenomenological Research*, Vol. 19, 1958.

McKeon, R. (1951a): Philosophy and Method, in *Journal of Philosophy*, Vol. 48, 1951.

McKeon, R. (ed.) (1951b): *Democracy in a World of Tensions: A Symposium Prepared by UNESCO*. Chicago, The University of Chicago Press, 1951.

Mead, M. (1952): How an Anthropologist Writes, in *Male and Female: A Study of the Sexes in a Changing World*. New York, William Morrow & Co., 1952.

Mei, Y. (1929): *The Ethical and Political Works of Motse*. London, Probsthain Press, 1929.

Meinecke, F. (1933): Kausalitäten und Werte in der Geschichte, in *Staat und Persönlichkeit*. Berlin, E. S. Mittler & Sohn, 1933.

Merleau-Ponty, M. (1953): *Éloge de la philosophie*. Paris, Librairie Gallimard, 1953.

Merton, R. K. (1938): Social Structure and Anomie, in *American Sociological Review*, Vol. 3, 1938.

Merton, R. K. (1941): (Review of) Znaniecki's *The Social Role of the Man of Knowledge*, in *American Sociological Review*, Vol. 6, 1941.

Merton, R. K. (1945): The Sociology of Knowledge, in *Twentieth Century Sociology*, ed. Gurvitch and Moore. New York, The Philosophical Library, 1945.

Merton, R. K. (1957): *Social Theory and Social Structure* (revised second edition). Glencoe, The Free Press, 1957.

Michels, R. (1912): *Political Parties: A Sociological Study of the Oligarchical Tendencies of Modern Democracy.* Glencoe, The Free Press, 1949.

Michels, R. (1927): *First Lectures in Political Sociology (Corso di Sociologia Politica),* trans. Alfred Da Grazia, Jr. Minneapolis, University of Minnesota Press, 1949.

Mills, C. W. (1940): Methodological Consequences of the Sociology of Knowledge, in *Am. J. Sociology,* Vol. 46, 1940.

Mills, C. W. (1956): *The Power Elite.* New York, Oxford University Press, 1957.

Mills, C. W. (1959): *The Sociological Imagination.* New York, Oxford University Press, 1959.

Misch, G. (1924): Einleitung, *Diltheys Gesammelte Schriften,* Vol. V. Leipzig and Berlin, B. G. Teubner, 1924.

Misch, G. (1951): *The Dawn of Philosophy: A Philosophical Primer (Der Weg in die Philosophie),* ed. R. F. C. Hull. Cambridge, Harvard University Press, 1951.

Mises, R. v. (1951): *Positivism: A Study in Human Understanding (Kleines Lehrbuch des Positivismus),* trans. J. Bernstein and R. G. Newton. Cambridge, Harvard University Press, 1951.

Moore, G. E. (1922): *Principia Ethica: The Subject Matter of Ethics.* Cambridge, Cambridge University Press, 1922.

Moore, S. W. (1957): *The Critique of Capitalist Democracy: An Introduction to the Theory of the State in Marx, Engels and Lenin.* New York, Paine-Whitman, 1957.

More, T. (1516): Utopia: The Discourse of Raphael Hythloday, of the Best State of a Commonwealth, in *Famous Utopias of the Renaissance,* ed. F. R. White. New York, Packard & Co., 1946.

Morgenthau, H. J. (1948): *Politics Among Nations: The Struggle for Power and Peace* (third revised edition). New York, Alfred A. Knopf, 1960.

Muensterberger, A. and Axelrod, S. (eds.) (1947-58): *Psychoanalysis and the Social Sciences* (founded by Géza Róheim). New York, International Universities Press, 1947-1958 (cf. esp. Vol. 5)

Myrdal, G. (1944): *An American Dilemma: The Negro Problem and Modern Democracy.* New York, Harper & Bros., 1944.

Myrdal, G. (1958): *Value in Social Theory.* New York, Harper & Bros., 1958.

Naess, A., Christopherson, J. A. and Kval, K. (1956): *Democracy, Ideology and Objectivity: Studies in the Semantics and Cognitive Analysis of Ideological Controversy.* Oslo, Oslo University Press, 1956,

Nagel, E. (1936): Impression and Appraisals of Analytic Philosophy in Europe, in *The Journal of Philosophy*, Vol. 33, 1936.

Nagel, E. (1944): Logic Without Ontology, in *Naturalism and the Human Spirit*, ed. Y. H. Krikorian. New York, Columbia University Press, 1944.

Nagel, E. (1954): *Sovereign Reason, and other Studies in the Philosophy of Science*. Glencoe, The Free Press, 1954.

Nagel, E. (1957): A Formalization of Functionalism, in *Logic Without Metaphysics, and other Essays in the Philosophy of Science*. Glencoe, The Free Press, 1957.

Nagel, E. (1960): Determinism in History, in *Philosophy and Phenomenological Research*, Vol. 20, 1960.

Needham, J. (1956): *Science and Civilization in China (History of Scientific Thought*, Vol. 2). Cambridge, Cambridge University Press, 1956.

Nettler, G. (1945): A Test For The Sociology of Knowledge, in *American Sociological Review*, Vol. 10, 1945.

Nettler, G. (1957): A Measure of Alienation, in *American Sociological Review*, Vol. 22, 1957.

Neumann, F. L. (1957): *The Democratic and the Authoritarian State: Essays in Political and Legal Theory*. Glencoe, The Free Press, 1957.

Neurath, O. (1932): Sociology and Physicalism, reprinted in *Logical Positivism*, ed. A. J. Ayer (The Library of Philosophical Movements). Glencoe, The Free Press, 1959.

Neurath, O. (1944): *Foundations of the Social Sciences. International Encyclopedia of Unified Science*, Vol. II, No. 1. Chicago, University of Chicago Press, 1944.

Nietzsche, F. (1874): *The Use and Abuse of History*, trans. Adrian Collins. New York, The Liberal Arts Press, 1957.

Northrop, F. S. C. (1946): *The Meeting of East and West: An Inquiry Concerning World Understanding*. New York, The Macmillan Co., 1946.

Ornstein, M. (1928): *The Role of Scientific Societies in the Seventeenth Century* (revised second edition). Chicago, The University of Chicago Press, 1938.

Pareto, V. (1916): *The Mind and Society (Trattato di Sociologia Generale)*, trans. A. Livingston. New York, Harcourt, Brace & Co., 1935.

Parsons, T. (1937): *The Structure of Social Action: A Study in Social Theory with Special Reference to a Group of Recent European Writers*. New York, McGraw Hill Book Co., 1937.

Parsons, T. (1951a): *The Social System*. Glencoe, The Free Press, 1951.

Parsons, T. and Shils, E. (1951b): *Toward A General Theory of Action*. Cambridge, Harvard University Press, 1951.

Parsons, T. (1960): *Structure and Process in Modern Societies*. Glencoe, The Free Press, 1960.

156 PHILOSOPHY, SCIENCE AND THE SOCIOLOGY OF KNOWLEDGE

Passmore, J. A. (1958): The Objectivity of History, *Philosophy: Journal of the Royal Institute of Philosophy*, Vol. 33, 1958.

Plato (1892a): The Republic, in *The Dialogues of Plato* (2 vols.), trans. Benjamin Jowett. New York, The Macmillan Co., 1892.

Plato (1892b): Phaedrus, in *The Dialogues of Plato* (2 vols.), trans. Benjamin Jowett. New York, The Macmillan Co., 1892.

Plekhanov, G. (1895): *The Development of the Monist View of History.* trans. Andrew Rothstein. Moscow, Foreign Languages Publishing House, 1956.

Poincaré, H. (1913): *The Foundations of Science*, trans. G. B. Halstead. New York, The Science Press, 1913.

Polanyi, M. (1951): *The Logic of Liberty: Reflections and Rejoinders.* London, Routledge & Kegan Paul Ltd., 1951.

Popper, K. R. (1952): *The Open Society and Its Enemies* (second revised edition). London, Routledge & Kegan Paul Ltd., 1952.

Popper, K. R. (1957): The Unity of Method, in *The Poverty of Historicism*, Boston. The Beacon Press, 1957.

Pribram, K. (1949): *Conflicting Patterns of Thought.* Washington, D. C., Public Affairs Press, 1949.

Radin, P. (1927): *Primitive Man As Philosopher.* New York, D. Appleton & Co., 1927.

Radin, P. (1936): *Primitive Religion: Its Nature and Origin.* New York, The Viking Press, 1936.

Radin, P. (1953): *The World of Primitive Man.* New York, Henry Schuman Co., 1953.

Ramsey, F. P. (1931): *The Foundations of Mathematics.* London, Routledge & Kegan Paul, Ltd., 1931.

Rapoport, A. (1959): Anatol Rapoport, Uses and Limitations of Mathematical Models in Social Sciences, in *Symposium on Sociological Theory*, ed. Llewellyn Gross. *Loc. cit.*

Read, G. D. (1953): *Childbirth Without Fear: The Principles and Practice of Natural Childbirth* (revised and enlarged edition). Harper & Bros., New York, 1953.

Reich, W. (1925): *Der Triebhafte Charakter.* Int. Psa. Verlag, Vienna, 1925.

Reich, W. (1946): *The Mass Psychology of Fascism* (3rd ed.). New York, Orgone Institute Press, 1946.

Reichenbach, H. (1936): Logistic Empiricism in Germany and the Present State of Its Problems, in *Journal of Philosophy*, Vol. 33, 1936.

Reichenbach, H. (1951): The Functional Conception of Knowledge, in *The Rise of Scientific Philosophy.* Berkeley, University of California Press, 1951.

Richards, I. A. (1929): *Practical Criticism: A Study of Literary Judgment.* New York, Harcourt, Brace & Co., 1956.

Rickert, H. (1926): *Kulturwissenschaft und Naturwissenschaft.* Tübingen, J. C. B. Mohr, 1926.

Rieff, P. (1959): *Freud: The Mind of the Moralist.* New York, The Viking Press, 1959.

Riesman, D. (1950): *The Lonely Crowd: A Study of the Changing American Character.* New Haven, Yale University Press, 1950.

Riesman, D. (1954): *Individualism Reconsidered.* Glencoe, The Free Press, 1954.

Riesman, D. (1959): The College Professor, in *Education in the Age of Science,* ed. Brand Blanshard. New York, Basic Books, Inc., 1959.

Riessman, F. and Miller, S. M. (1959: Psychotherapy for Whom. *Bard Psychological J.,* Vol. I, No. 4, 1959.

Root, H. E. (1956): Introduction to Hume's *The Natural History of Religion.* London, Adam & Charles Black, 1956.

Rosenberg, B. (1958): *Mass Culture: The Popular Arts in America.* Glencoe, The Free Press, 1958.

Rosenberg, M. (1955): Faith in People and Success-Orientation, in *The Language of Social Research: A Reader in the Methodology of Social Research,* ed. Paul F. Lazarsfeld and Morris Rosenberg. Glencoe, The Free Press, 1955.

Ruyer, R. (1950): *L'Utopie et les utopistes.* Paris, Presses Universitaires de France, 1950.

Scheler, M. (1919): *Vom Umsturz der Werte.* Leipzig, Die Neue Geist-Verlag, 1923.

Scheler, M. (ed.) (1924): *Versuche zu einer Soziologie des Wissens.* Munich, Duncker & Humblot, 1924.

Scheler, M. (1926): *Die Wissensformen und die Gesellschaft: Probleme einer Soziologie des Wissens.* Leipzig, Die Neue Geist Verlag, 1926.

Scheler, M. (1927): *Der Formalismus in der Ethik und die Materiale Wertethik; neuer Versuch der Grundlegung eines ethischen Personalismus.* Halle, M. Niemeyer, 1927.

Scheler, M. (1928): *Die Stellung des Menschen im Kosmos.* Darmstadt, O. Reichl Verlag, 1928.

Schelting, A. von (1929): Zum Streit um die Wissenssoziologie, in *Archiv für Sozialwissenschaft und Sozialpolitik,* Vol. 62, 1929.

Schelting, A. von (1936): (Review of) Mannheim's *Ideologie und Utopie. American Sociological Review,* Vol. 1, 1936.

Schlesinger, R. (1945): *Soviet Legal Theory: Its Social Background and Development.* London, Routledge & Kegan Paul, Ltd., 1945.

Schücking, L. L. (1944): Shifting of the Sociological Position of the Artist, *The Sociology of Literary Taste*. New York, Oxford University Press, 1944.

Schumpeter, J. (1949): Science and Ideology, in *Essays of Joseph Schumpeter*, ed. R. V. Clemence. Cambridge, Addison-Wesley Press, 1951.

Scott, J. F. and Lynton, R. P. (1952): Developing the Systematic Knowledge of Social Understanding, in *The Community Factor in Modern Technology*. Paris, United Nations Educational, Scientific, and Cultural Organization, 1952.

Seeman, M. and Morris, R. T. (1950): The Problem of Leadership: An Interdisciplinary Approach, in *American Journal of Sociology*, Vol. 56, 1950.

Simmel, G. (1908): *Soziologie: Untersuchungen über die formen der Vergesellschaftung*, trans. Kurt H. Wolff, in *The Sociology of Georg Simmel*. Glencoe, The Free Press, 1950. See in this connection, Kurt H. Wolff, *Georg Simmel, 1858-1918: A Collection of Essays, with Translations and a Bibliography*. Columbus, The Ohio State University Press, 1959.

Sombart, W. (1918): *Die Juden und Das Wirtschaftsleben*. Munich and Leipzig, Duncker und Humblot, 1918.

Sombart, W. (1939): *Weltanschauung, Science and Economy*, trans. Philip Johnson. New York, Veritas Press, 1939.

Sorel, G. (1907): *Réflexions sur la violence*. Paris, Marcel Riviere (sixth edition), 1925.

Sorel, G. (1908): *La décomposition du Marxisme*. Paris, Marcel Rivière, 1910.

Sorokin, P. (1947): *Society, Culture and Personality: Their Structure and Dynamics*. New York, Harper & Bros., 1947.

Sorokin, P. (1951): *Social Philosophers of an Age of Crisis*. Boston, The Beacon Press, 1951.

Speier, H. (1952): *Social Order and the Risks of War: Papers in Political Sociology*. New York, George W. Stewart Publishers, 1952.

Stark, W. (1958): *The Sociology of Knowledge: An Essay in Aid of a Deeper Understanding of the History of Ideas*. London, Routledge and Kegan Paul, Ltd., 1958.

Strauss, L. (1959): *What Is Political Philosophy?* Glencoe, The Free Press, 1959.

Tawney, R. H. (1926): *Religion and the Rise of Capitalism*. New York, Harcourt, Brace & Co., 1926.

Toynbee, A. (1956): *An Historian's Approach to Religion*. London and New York, Oxford University Press, 1956.

Veblen, T. (1899): *The Theory of the Leisure Class: An Economic Study of Institutions*. New York, The Viking Press, 1931.

Veblen, T. (1918): *The Higher Learning in America: A Memorandum on the Conduct of Universities by Business Men*. New York, B. W. Huebsch, 1918.

Waley, A. (1939): *Three Ways of Thought in Ancient China*. New York, Doubleday & Co., 1956.

Watkins, J. W. N. (1953): Ideal Types and Historical Explanation, in *Readings in the Philosophy of Science*, ed. H. Feigl and M. Brodbeck. New York, Appleton-Century-Crofts, 1953.

Weber, A. (1934): *Kulturgeschichte als Kultursoziologie*. Leiden, Sitthoff, 1934.

Weber, A. (1948): *Farewell to European History, or the Conquest of Nihilism*. New Haven, Yale University Press, 1948.

Weber, M. (1904): *The Protestant Ethic and the Spirit of Capitalism*, trans. Talcott Parsons. New York, Charles Scribner's Sons, 1958.

Weber, M. (1919): Politics as a Vocation, in *From Max Weber: Essays in Sociology*, trans. H. Gerth and C. W. Mills. New York, Oxford Univ. Press, 1946.

Weber, M. (1921): Vorwort zum dritten Band (Marianne Weber, in *Gesammelte Aufsätze zur Religionssoziologie*, Vol. III: *Das antike Judentum*. Tübingen, J. C. B. Mohr (Paul Siebeck), 1921.

Weber M. (1924): Objectivity in Social Science, in *The Methodology of the Social Sciences*, trans. E. A. Shils and H. A. Finch. Glencoe, The Free Press, 1949.

Weber, M. (1947): The Types of Authority and Imperative Co-ordination, in *The Theory of Social and Economic Organization*, trans. A. M. Henderson and Talcott Parsons. New York, Oxford University Press, 1947.

Weber, M. (1950): *General Economic History (Wirtschaftsgeschichte)*, trans. Frank H. Knight. Glencoe, The Free Press, 1950.

Weiner, P. P. (1949): *Evolution and the Founders of Pragmatism*. Cambridge, Harvard University Press, 1949.

Westfall, R. S. (1958): *Science and Religion in Seventeenth Century England*. New Haven, Yale University Press, 1958.

Wetter, G. A. (1952): *Dialectical Materialism: A Historical and Systematic Survey of Philosophy in the Soviet Union*, trans. Peter Heath. London, Routledge & Kegan Paul, Ltd., 1958.

Weyl, T. (1949): *Philosophy of Mathematics and Natural Science*. Princeton, Princeton University Press, 1949.

Wild, J. (1953): *Plato's Modern Enemies and the Theory of Natural Law*. Chicago, The University of Chicago Press, 1953.

Wilson, L. (1942): *The Academic Man*. New York, Oxford University Press, 1942.

Winspear, A. D. (1940): *The Genesis of Plato's Thought*. New York, Dryden Press, 1940.

Wirth, L. (1940): Ideological Aspects of Social Disorganization, in *Am. Sociological Review*, Vol. 5, 1940.

Wittgenstein, L. (1953): *Philosophical Investigations (Philosophische Untersuchungen)*, trans. G. E. M. Anscombe. Oxford, Basil Blackwell, 1953.

Wolff, K. H. (1943): The Sociology of Knowledge: Emphasis on an Empirical Attitude, in *Philosophy of Science*, Vol. 10, 1943.

Wolff, K. H. (1946): *The Sociology of Knowledge: A Study and a Theory.* (Graduate Seminar Conducted at The Ohio State University, Columbus, Ohio) Mimeographed copy, privately distributed, 1946.

Wolff, K. H. (1959): The Sociology of Knowledge and Sociological Theory, in *Symposium on Sociological Theory*, ed. Lewellyn Gross. *loc.sit.*

Yinger, J. M. (1957): *Religion, Society and the Individual: An Introduction to the Sociology of Religion.* New York, The Macmillan Co., 1957.

Zetterberg, H. (1954): On Axiomatic Theories in Sociology, in *The Language of Social Research: A Reader in the Methodology of Social Research*, ed. Paul F. Lazarsfeld and Morris Rosenberg. Glencoe, The Free Press, 1955.

Zilsel, E. (1941): Physics and the Problem of Historico-Sociological Laws, in *Philosophy of Science*, Vol. 8, 1941.

Zilsel, E. (1942): The Sociological Roots of Science, in *Am. J. Sociology*, Vol. 47, 1942.

Zilsel, E. (1945): The Genesis of the Concept of Scientific Progress, in *Journal of the History of Ideas*, Vol. 6, 1945.

Znaniecki, F. (1940): *The Social Role of the Man of Knowledge.* New York, Columbia University Press, 1940.

Znaniecki, F. (1951): The Present and the Future of the Sociology of Knowledge, in *Soziologische Forschung in unserer Zeit*, ed. Karl Specht. Koln-Opladen, Westdeutscher Verlag, 1951.

Name Index

161

Lavine, T. Z., 64, 150
Lazarsfeld, P. F., 36, 109, 111, 129, 150
Lee, O., 42, 150
Lefebvre, H., 42, 150
Lenin, V. I., 82-3, 103, 151
Lenzen, V. F., 69, 151
Leroy, M., 57
Lessing, G. E., 32, 126
Levinson, D. J., vii, 68, 151
Levinson, R., 15, 151
Lévy-Bruhl, L., 25, 86, 151
Lewin, K., 120, 121, 151
Lewis, J., 151
Likert, R., 109, 151
Lin Ching-Hsi, 12
Lippitt, R., 109, 151
Lipset, S. M., 66, 151
Liu Shao, 11
Lobatchevski, N. I., 44
Locke, J., 26, 28, 85
Lowenthal, L., 151
Lucretius, 14-18, 151
Lukacs, G., 45, 76, 152
Lundberg, G. A., 52, 152
Lützeler, H., 152
Lynton, R. P., 158

M

Mach, E., 44
Machiavelli, N., 13, 66
Malebranche, N., 24-8, 152
Malinowski, B., 80f, 152
Mandelbaum, M., 10, 77, 152
Mannheim, K., v, 10, 11, 31, 36, 40, 41, 63-4, 75-6, 82, 85, 90, 96-7ff, 127, 128, 152
Maquet, J. J., vi, 140, 152
Marcel, G., 56
Marcuse, H., 30, 74, 96f, 152
Maritain, J., 101, 153
Marquis, D. G., 153
Martindale, D., 122, 153
Marx, K., vi, 3, 10, 11, 18, 32-3, 38, 46, 65, 79, 82, 85, 87, 122, 126, 153
Maxwell, W., 44
Mayer, J. P., 153
McGee, R. J., 129, 142
McGlynn, J. V., 57, 153
McKeon, R., 42, 153

Mead, M., 153
Mei, Y., 153
Meinecke, F., 139, 153
Mendelssohn, M., 32
Merleau-Ponty, M., 57, 153
Merton, R. K., v, 4, 8, 36, 54, 112-19, 138, 153, 154
Michels, R., 66, 72, 83, 139, 154
Mill, J. S., 85
Miller, S. M., 74, 157
Mills, C. W., 53, 66, 112, 154
Misch, G., 10, 154
Mises, R. v., 43, 154
Moore, G. E., 154
Moore, S. W., 45, 154
More, T., 90, 92, 154
Morgenthau, H. J., 134, 154
Morris, R. T., 118, 158
Mosca, G., 11, 72, 98, 99
Motse, 13
Muensterberger, A., 68, 154
Myrdal, G., 65, 154

N

Naess, A., 129, 154
Nagel, E., 44, 49, 54, 112, 113-15, 125, 155
Needham, J., 8, 12, 155
Nettler, G., 89, 129, 155
Neumann, F. L., 72, 155
Neurath, O., 70, 109, 155
Newton, I., 22, 34, 44
Nietzsche, F., 10, 11, 32, 67, 124, 125, 131, 155
Northrop, F. S. C., 155
Novikoff, A., 108

O

Oppenheim, P., 57, 148
Ornstein, M., 155
Orwell, G., 95, 96f
Owen, R., 92

P

Pareto, V., 11, 40, 66, 72, 83, 97, 98, 139, 155
Parsons, T., v, 39, 112, 114, 118, 121, 138, 155
Passmore, J. A., 124, 156
Pavlov, I., 34

Subject Index

A
Alienation, 33, 45, 65
Anomie, 138
Anthropology
philosophical, 32, 33
physical, 44
Apriori constructs, 28, 35
Atheism, 22
Authority, 81-2, 100

B
Behaviour
action and, 83, 122
general theory of, 6, 101, 120, 122
measurement of, 63, 110, 121
political, 66
Belief
and repression, 74, 101-21
validation of, 74, 84, 110-11
Biology, 113-14, 120
Brave New World, 4

C
Charisma, 22, 138
Chinese thought, 11-14
Christianity, 32, 33, 85
Civitas Solis, 92
Class, 15, 16, 68
Coercion, 98-105 passim
Confucianism, 11-14
Consciousness
false, 18, 81, 82, 86
and ideology, 10
and social class, 20
true, 81, 86
types of, 18
Conventionalism, 29, 38, 43, 135
Counter-ideology (see also Ideology)
definition of, 88-9
production of, 39, 87-9
role of, 89, 91
Counter-Utopia, 95-6 see also Utopianism
Critique of Pure Reason, 28

D
De l'esprit, 25, 26
De l'homme, 27
De Rerum Natura, 16
Democracy, 85
Determinism, 68, 120, 125-6, 131, 135
Dialectics
logic of, 42
materialism and, 46
as social force, 45-6
Dualism, 5, 38, 85

E
Economics
attitudes towards, 71
and ideology, 64, 65
and sociology, 65
Elite
definition of, 138-9
empirical typology of, 66, 98-9
and masses, 16, 46, 99, 103
and problem of knowledge, 16, 75-6,
83-4, 100-5
Empiricism, 12, 24, 28, 47, 53
Encyclopedism, 24, 28
Enlightenment, 23, 28, 32, 75, 100, 126,
136
Epistemology, 18, 24, 26, 34-5, 115, 123
Essence of Christianity (The), 32
Estrangement, see Alienation
Existentialism, 3, 108, 124

F
Field Theory, 107, 120-22
Fin de siècle, 4, 7, 73
Freedom
and coercion, 74-5, 99, 100
and order, 94
and political repression, 75
and society, 75
Freischwebende Intelligenz, 96
French Revolution, 8

165

DATE DUE

JAN 2 9 1987		